WIND, WATER, AND, FIRE

ALSO BY NIKOLAS LARUM

Non-fiction
*The Blood of Jesus Christ: Its Life to the Body, Its Power for the
Priesthood, and Its Purchase of the Bride*

Fiction
Gypsy Spy: The Cold War Files

WIND, WATER, AND FIRE

Understanding the Holy Spirit through Biblical Symbolism

by Nikolas Larum

C P

CARLISLE PUBLISHING, LLC
CHEASAPEAKE

Wind, Water, and Fire: Understanding the Holy Spirit through Biblical Symbolism
by Nikolas Larum

Copyright © 2018 by Nikolas Larum
Carlisle Publishing, LLC, Chesapeake 23321
Published 2018

ISBN 978-0-9998850-1-7

DEDICATION

ಬೋಚ

In memory of my father, John Harold Larum, who was a living demonstration of how Christ loved the church and who, in his dying days, admonished me to keep my heart open to the Lord and get "my head in the Book." I love you, Dad!

Contents

ଚଚଓ

ILLUSTRATIONS

᠍ഔൽ

Figures

Tables

Relating to an Invisible God

The Godhead is ponderously difficult to grapple with. We, after all, are finite creatures in a material world. And the task before us is to have a meaningful relationship with the omnipotent, omniscient, eternal, and invisible Creator of the universe. No small feat. But, of course, He knows that.

God planted the Garden of Eden to provide the perfect place for man to commune with Him. Fellowship is what He had in mind when He created us. Certainly, the problem of the relational disparity between an infinite being and a finite race must have occurred to Him. So how did the invisible God decide to show Himself to mankind?

Romans 1:20
For ever since the creation of the world His invisible nature and attributes, that is, His eternal power and divinity, have been made intelligible and clearly discernible in and through the things that have been made (His handiworks). So [men] are without excuse [altogether without any defense or justification], AMP

He surrounded us with a witness of Himself in the created order. The nearest, most tangible reality of the created order for us humans is family. Even orphans are born from somebody. Family ties, though not universally experienced, are universally known. Thus, the Persons of the Godhead are made known to us through familial terms: God the Father, God the Son, and God the Holy Spirit. God the Holy Spirit?

What part of the family tree is that? "Father" I understand. The term is full of emotional imprint and real life imagery. "Son" is equally comprehensible. I have four of them. In addition to this vertical term of relationship for the Second Person, we have also been given a horizontal one: brother. That speaks to me. I have five of them. But when it comes to the Spirit of God, the terminology leaves us grasping the air in our attempt to relate to Him. How do you hug a spirit?

Thoughts similar to these were afflicting me as I was driving home from work one day years ago. As I downshifted and moved to the left-hand lane to make a turn, the Holy Spirit dropped a project in my heart. Thankful for a red light for once in my life, I scribbled down the impressions I was receiving as fast as I could in the back of a book that was on the passenger seat. The light turned green and I turned left. Little did I know that those short eighteen lines of notes jotted down in less than half a minute would occupy me for the next ten months while I fleshed them out. He's that way. He always gives us more than we think we have.

The premise is simple. It comes straight from Romans 1:20. The created things teach us about the Creator. But not haphazardly. Exactly how the lessons of the creation are to be applied to the Godhead is codified for us in Scripture through symbolism. Thus, the Father is the Potter[1], The Son is the Lamb and the Lion[2], and the Holy Spirit is— well, that's what this book is all about.

We humans are generally either too compartmentalized or too reductionist or, worse yet, both. Did I mention that we were finite? The sheer volume of information assaulting us at any given moment forces us to parse it down continually just to cope. No wonder then that we like silver-bullet remedies, the-butler-did-it mysteries, and straight forward cause-and-effect histories. The wonder drug that cures it all,

---

[1] Isa. 64:8.
[2] Rev. 5:5-6.

lone gunman theories, and the singular causes of war are all attractive because of their simplicity. But we all know that real life is much more complex than that. Life's Creator is no different.

In painting a picture of Himself, the Holy Spirit wasn't content to be cast in singular hues. He has far too many dimensions to His personality for monochromatic expressions to do Him justice. His infiniteness required symbolic language that on the surface appears contradictory but in actuality works to provide us a glimpse of the breadth, length, depth, and height of His Being. Thus, He is wind and cloud, water and fire, oil and lamp, dove and eagle, to name a few. It is through this language of symbol that we are enabled to begin to grapple with the Third Person of the Trinity.

How do you hug a spirit? Better to ask how the Spirit hugs you. It is my earnest hope and desire that you feel His embrace as you read this work.

CHAPTER 1

God the Holy Spirit

The ever-speaking partner of the Godhead

Writers are strange creatures, often stretched between the polar opposites of holding opinions and dreams so strong that they must be written down and emotions too fragile to handle editorial comments. I'm no different. I have my convictions. But I want approval. These things are often mutually exclusive. Fully aware of my frailty, I called my mother on the phone and read to her the introduction to this book (the one you just read—unless, of course, you happen to be a skip reader. Did you like the conclusion?). "What do you think?" I asked. "Amazing," she said, "for someone who never used to believe in the Trinity." Ouch.

Shocked? She was right. Well, nearly right. I was brought up on the knees of the Southern Baptist faith, so denial of the Trinity hadn't always been a part of my confession. But in my early teens, I got entangled in a Unitarian cult.[3] After ten years of indoctrination, the Lord delivered me from that organization. What followed was a long journey of reexamining some of the basic tenants of Christianity: life after death, the anointing work of the Holy Spirit, and the nature of the Godhead. What I discovered on this journey, among other things, was that many Christians accept basic theological tenets at face value without ever bothering to ferret them out in Scripture. Though their

---

[3] Not to be confused with Unitarian Universalists. This was a Unitarian "Christian" cult.

faith is commendable, it is in that condition rendered indefensible. Without the word of God as a sure foundation to stand on, how are they to combat the doctrinal errors propagated by the enemy?

I do not regard myself to be an expert on the Trinity. If I had to define the progression of my theology, I would have to say that I have moved from Ignorance (or simple conformity) to Unitarianism (or straight-forward deception) to Trinitarianism (or informed ignorance). Ortho-doxy's embrace can be an elusive thing. Just when you think you are in the fold, there are still those who wish to inform you that you are from the wrong flock! A simple, cursory read of the Trinitarian debate throughout Church history, past and present, is sufficient to show that even Trinitarians have had a hard time agreeing on all the particulars of what constitutes orthodoxy.

If the nature of the Trinity has never intrigued or baffled you, I'll war-rant that you haven't given it much thought. The problem with this "take it on faith" approach is that it leaves one very vulnerable to false doctrines regarding the Godhead. Though various groups have denied the divinity of Jesus Christ in many different ways since the days of His earthly ministry, most saints will flatly reject any notion that He is not God. The same goes for any claim that YHWH, the Father, isn't God. Where ignorance regarding the nature of the Godhead is most destructive to the body of Christ (because it affects the largest amount of people) is in our understanding of the Holy Spirit.

I was held captive for many years in a system of faith that denied the divinity of Jesus Christ. For this unorthodox belief, the group I was a part of was rightly classified as a cult by the greater body of Christ. But many of these same God-fearing folks who righteously branded me and my companions with the big "C" would talk about and relate to the Holy Spirit as if He were an impersonal force. These things should not be. If we are to have a complete and battle-worthy theology of the Godhead, we must be clear on who and what the Holy Spirit is.

As I have already stated, I do not claim to be an expert. I claim the position of informed ignorance. This leaves me great room for learning. If some of the concepts in this chapter (or this book, for that matter) seem heretical to the reader, forgive me. It is not my intent to offend, only to inform. All I ask is that you "search the Scriptures to see if these things are so."[4] And though it is true that we may never agree on all the particulars of orthodoxy in this life, we must agree that the Godhead is an awesome and mysterious Entity.

1 Timothy 3:16
And without controversy great is the mystery of godliness: God was manifest in the flesh, justified in the Spirit, seen of angels, preached unto the Gentiles, believed on in the world, received up into glory.

Exact Identity
Romans 1:20
For the invisible things of him from the creation of the world are clearly seen, being understood by the things that are made, even his eternal power and Godhead; so that they are without excuse:

God speaks to us through the creation. This is the whole crux of symbolism. "A symbol [in Scripture]…is designed to represent certain characteristics or qualities in that which it represents. To be interpreted, it requires a pointing out of the characteristics, qualities, marks or features **common** to both the symbol and that which it symbolizes."[5] To understand the God we cannot see, we must study the creation that we can see. The whole creation gives evidence of God. That is what this book is all about. We are going to examine what the Holy Spirit wants us to understand about Him when He calls Himself a river, or a dove, or an eagle, or a cloud, or oil.

---

[4] Acts 17:11.
[5] Kevin Connor, *Interpreting the Symbols and Types*, BT Publishing, Portland, OR, 1992, p. 85. Emphasis added.

Now, I'll admit that the simplistic definition of the Trinity sounds illogical: three Persons, individual, yet unified; each God, but not three gods. How can this be? It sounds entirely illogical. Our claim to Monotheism is challenged by Jews and Muslims alike in the face of our Trinitarian confession "You can't have Three Persons being God and claim to believe in only One God," they say. But we do.

Suppose you had two oxygen atoms, each at the same temperature and pressure. In other words, they are in the same quantum state. Can these two atoms be distinguished? No, from the quantum mechanics point of view, they are the same atom. If you interchanged them physically, the universe is unchanged. Without this exact identity, there would be no stability of matter and keeping track of chemical reactions would be impossible.[6] So we see that even on an atomic scale, two things (or three) can be one. Why would anyone think this to be an impossibility with God?

Not only the principle of exact identity, but also the pervasive state of interdependence in the creation, speaks to us of the Godhead. George Otis, Jr., states it this way:

> "The truth of the matter is that God's universe has operated on the principle of interdependence from the very beginning. Atomic structure, the human body, and the family unit all testify to this truth. From one end of creation to the other, nothing is strong enough or sufficient enough to operate with total autonomy. The strategy is delightfully coherent: Let material creation reflect the intrinsic interdependence of the Trinity, and then encourage moral creation to take note and emulate the divine pattern."[7]

---

[6] Frank J. Tipler, *The Physics of Immortality*, Doubleday, New York, NY, 1994, p. 230.
[7] George Otis, Jr., *The Last of the Giants*, Baker Book House Co., Grand Rapids, MI, 1991, p. 232.

Father, Son, and Spirit Are the Same

Far be it from me to try to reduce the Godhead to a quantum level. But if two systems of the same substance in the same quantum state are indistinguishable, what about Three Persons in the same God state? If these Three Persons be shown to have the same essence, powers, attributes, and privileges, would they not, in a sense, be indistinguishable?

The same God state? Herein lies the power in the term Godhead versus Trinity. For one, Godhead happens to be found in the Bible, whereas Trinity is strictly a theological term of human invention. We use the term Godhead like the name of a governing council. For instance, "The Triumvirate determined that the empire should be shared." Or, "The Council met today to decide next year's budget." In this sense, I think the term Godhead is much more useful and less confusing than Trinity. Be that as it may, our use of it in this way confuses us with regard to its true meaning.

The English word "godhead" comes from the Middle English *god-hede*: GOD + *hede*, which is a variant of *–hode*, or as we see it today, -HOOD. Thus, our word "Godhead" does not speak to position but to the state, condition, or quality of being. It means Godhood. The Father, Son, and Holy Spirit all have Godhood: The state, condition, and quality of being God.

The term "Godhead" appears only three times in the King James Version (KJV), and each time it is a translation of a different Greek word as is shown in Figure 1.1.

The verses from 2 Peter teach us that we can share in the nature of divinity. Through His power and promises, God imparts to us the ability to manifest His likeness, to take on "Godlikeness" or "Godhood." If this statement makes you nervous, then spit a curse at the spirit of religion in the name of Jesus Christ. Being in God's likeness was the purpose of our creation and redemption.

Romans 1:20 teaches us that we understand the power and majesty of God through the observation of His works. The third use of Godhead in the KJV comes closest to the way we use it the most.

Colossians 2:9
For in him dwelleth all the fulness of the Godhead [theotes] *bodily.*

The term *theotes* means God's personality as directly revealed. This verse teaches us that all that it means to be God (the full expression of Godhood) dwells bodily in our Lord Jesus Christ. This is the preeminent revelation of the New Testament. Thus, Father, Son, and Holy Spirit are in the same God state. They have the same essence, attributes, power, and privileges.

16

In essence, the Father, Son, and Holy Spirit are the same. All three are spirit.[8] All three are the Word.[9] As the Spirit, they have life in and of themselves and provide life to all else. As the Word, they define the reality of all existence.[10]

They are the same in attributes. The Father, Son, and Holy Spirit are all eternal, without beginning or end.

Isaiah 9:6
For unto us a child is born, unto us a son is given: and the government shall be upon his shoulder: and his name shall be called Wonderful, Counsellor, The mighty God, The everlasting Father, The Prince of Peace.

This is one of the many verses giving a Trinitarian witness of the Godhead in the Old Testament. The prophecy is about Jesus, the child born, the son given. But note the names the Son is given: Wonderful Counselor, everlasting Father. The Holy Spirit is called the Spirit of counsel in Isaiah 11:2. And the Father is everlasting.

Psalms 90:2
Before the mountains were brought forth, or ever thou hadst formed the earth and the world, even from everlasting to everlasting, thou art God.

Those who argue against the divinity of Jesus do so on these very same eternal grounds. Since he was born, he had a beginning; thus he cannot be God, they reason. But they are wrong. It isn't that He had a beginning. It is that He *is* the Beginning.

---

[8] John 4:24 God [the Father] is Spirit. Acts 2:36 declares that Jesus is Lord and Christ and 2 Cor. 3:17 states that the Lord is Spirit. The Holy Spirit, of course, is Himself Spirit (Rom. 8:16).
[9] John 1:1, 14; 6:63.
[10] Heb. 1:3 among others.

Revelation 22:13
I am Alpha and Omega, the beginning and the end, the first and the last.

The title of Alpha and Omega (one which the Father bears as well in Hebrew as the Aleph and the Tau) is a claim to sovereignty over time. Only One outside of time can claim rulership over it. It is an eternal epithet. And the eternal Son offered Himself to the eternal Father through the eternal Spirit.

Hebrews 9:14
How much more shall the blood of Christ, who through the eternal Spirit offered himself without spot to God, purge your conscience from dead works to serve the living God?

Not only are they all eternal. They are all also omniscient. This means that they know everything and cannot be taught anything.

Psalms 147:5
Great is our Lord, and of great power: his understanding is infinite.

1 John 3:20
For if our heart condemn us, God is greater than our heart, and knoweth all things.

The above verses declare the omniscience of the Father. As the saying goes, like Father, like Son.

Hebrews 4:12-14
12 For the word of God is quick, and powerful, and sharper than any twoedged sword, piercing even to the dividing asunder of soul and spirit, and of the joints and marrow, and is a discerner of the thoughts and intents of the heart.

13 Neither is there any creature that is not manifest in his sight: but all things are naked and opened unto the eyes of him with whom we have to do.

14 Seeing then that we have a great high priest, that is passed into the heavens, Jesus the Son of God, let us hold fast our profession.

I know that many of us are accustomed to applying verse 12 to the written word of God. And though it is true that the written word is powerful, these verses are speaking of the Living Word, the Lord Jesus Christ. He is the One with whom we have to do and from whom nothing is hidden. He sees all. He knows all.

Colossians 2:2-3

2 That their hearts might be comforted, being knit together in love, and unto all riches of the full assurance of understanding, to the acknowledgement of the mystery of God, and of the Father, and of Christ;

3 In whom are hid all the treasures of wisdom and knowledge.

In Christ are hidden all the treasures of wisdom and knowledge. He is omniscient and so is the Spirit.

1 Corinthians 2:10-11

10 But God hath revealed them unto us by his Spirit: for the Spirit searcheth all things, yea, the deep things of God.

11 For what man knoweth the things of a man, save the spirit of man which is in him? even so the things of God knoweth no man, but the Spirit of God.

If you were to meet someone who had the exact same knowledge set as you did (i.e., they would have the exact same memories, skills, opinions, perspectives, etc.), who would that person be? Well, who besides you has the *exact* same thoughts you do? Nobody. In that all Three Persons of the Godhead are omniscient, they all have the exact same knowledge set. This alone would make them One. But not only are all Three omniscient, they are also omnipresent.

Jeremiah 23:23-24
23 Am I a God at hand, saith the LORD, and not a God afar off?
24 Can any hide himself in secret places that I shall not see him? saith the LORD. Do not I fill heaven and earth? saith the LORD.

YHWH is the Father's name. In the King James Version (as well as several others), the translators have tried to tip us off to the use of YHWH in the original text by translating it as LORD in all caps. No one can hide from God the Father for He is everywhere.

Ephesians 4:10
He Who descended is the [very] same as He Who also has ascended high above all the heavens, that He [His presence] might fill all things (the whole universe, from the lowest to the highest). AMP

The Lord Jesus Christ is omnipresent.[11] Was He omnipresent during His earthly ministry? No, He willingly left heaven and submitted to being confined to the singularity of a human body that veiled His divinity.[12] After His ascension, He was glorified to His former position and entered once again into the omniscient and omnipresent state of Godhood.[13]

---

[11] See also Eph. 1:20-23 and Col. 1:15-17.
[12] See Phil. 2:5-7 and Heb. 10:20.
[13] There are those who would take umbrage at this idea, concerned that any loss of either would mean that He wasn't fully God. Jesus never ceased being fully God. As the verses in Phil. 2:5-7 explain, He willingly laid down these qualities and took on the form of a servant [in form, man; in substance, God]. This explains the different state of knowledge He had from the Father while on earth (Mark 13:32) as well as His prayer to be glorified to His former state (John 17:5). This glorification was a prerequisite for the outpouring of the Holy Spirit (John 7:39).

Psalms 139:7-8

7 Whither shall I go from thy spirit? or whither shall I flee from thy presence?

8 If I ascend up into heaven, thou art there: if I make my bed in hell, behold, thou art there.

If you can't hide from it, it's everywhere. The Spirit of God is omnipresent. Even those in hell can't hide from Him. He has what you might call a pervasive Presence. I don't know how folks in hell feel about it, but it is certainly good news for us. What plans, schemes, or machinations can the hordes of hell hide from our Holy God? None. God has never been surprised by anything the devil has ever done. Saddened, yes. Surprised, no.

So far, we have seen that the Father, Son, and Holy Spirit are of the same essence (Spirit and Word) and have the same attributes (eternal, omniscient, and omnipresent). Their power is also of the same quality and quantity. It is omnipotent.

Isaiah 26:4
Trust ye in the LORD for ever: for in the LORD JEHOVAH is everlasting strength:

Matthew 19:26
But Jesus beheld them, and said unto them, With men this is impossible; but with God all things are possible.

The Father's strength is everlasting and nothing is impossible with Him. The Son and the Spirit share in His might.

Revelation 1:8
I am Alpha and Omega, the beginning and the ending, saith the Lord, which is, and which was, and which is to come, the Almighty.

Job 33:4
The Spirit of God hath made me, and the breath of the Almighty hath
given me life.

The Lord Jesus Christ calls Himself the Almighty and the Spirit of
God is called the breath of the Almighty. His hand is never too short to
accomplish what is required.[14] As the Omnipotent, Omnipresent, Omniscient, and Eternal God, He holds the unique right and privilege of
being worshipped. Much is worshipped that is not God. But only He is
worthy of it.

Exodus 20:3-6
3 Thou shalt have no other gods before me.
4 Thou shalt not make unto thee any graven image, or any likeness of
  any thing that is in heaven above, or that is in the earth beneath, or
  that is in the water under the earth:
5 Thou shalt not bow down thyself to them, nor serve them: for I the
  LORD thy God am a jealous God, visiting the iniquity of the fathers
  upon the children unto the third and fourth generation of them that
  hate me;
6 And shewing mercy unto thousands of them that love me, and keep
  my commandments.

That the Father is to receive worship is not really open to debate.
Where arguments have risen throughout the course of church history is
whether the Son and the Holy Spirit are to be worshipped. For instance, Paul of Samosata, Patriarch of Antioch at the end of the third
century, would not allow prayer to Jesus Christ in his church or hymns
in Christ's honor. The Father alone was to be worshipped, and prayers
were to be *through* Christ, as intermediary between God and man.[15]

---

[14] See Num. 11:23 and Mic. 2:7.
[15] Joan O'Grady, *Early Christian Heresies*, Barnes & Noble Books, New York, 1985, p.
87.

If some would treat the Son this way, what of the supposed silent partner of the Trinity? Because many hold to the concept (either in practice or by tenet) of the Holy Spirit as an impersonal force, worshipping Him seems at best weird and at worst unbiblical. I can't help much with the weirdness aspect, but hopefully I can cast some light on the subject through Biblical documentation.

Matthew 14:33
Then they that were in the ship came and worshipped him, saying, Of a truth thou art the Son of God.

Never does Christ reprove anybody for worshipping Him. How could He since the Father commands it?

Hebrews 1:6
And again, when he bringeth in the firstbegotten into the world, he saith, And let all the angels of God worship him.

Philippians 2:9-11
9 Wherefore God also hath highly exalted him, and given him a name which is above every name:
10 That at the name of Jesus every knee should bow, of things in heaven, and things in earth, and things under the earth;
11 And that every tongue should confess that Jesus Christ is Lord, to the glory of God the Father.

Those who argue against the direct worship of the Holy Spirit do so on the grounds of a supposed lack of proof text. Where is the verse that says "Worship the Holy Spirit?" they ask. Glad you asked.

Revelation 19:10
And I fell at his feet to worship him. And he said unto me, See thou do it not: I am thy fellowservant, and of thy brethren that have the testimony of Jesus: **worship God***: for the testimony of Jesus is the spirit of prophecy.* [Emphasis added.]

23

Worship God! End of story. The very fact that any would argue against worshipping the Holy Spirit is evidence of a belief that He isn't fully God. If the Holy Spirit be God, then worship Him we must. If we refuse to worship Him, then our actions confess that we do not truly believe that He is God. It really is that simple. But though a soft answer may turn away wrath, simple explanations don't always quell a debate. For those who prefer a longer logic chain, what follows is for you.

Worshipping the Holy Spirit
In a concordance search of the KJV for the terms "worship" and "spirit" appearing in the same verse, one would only find four references: John 4:23-24, Philippians 3:3, and Revelation 19:10. In all of these, the closest we get to "Worship the Holy Spirit" is John 4:24.

John 4:24
God is a Spirit: and they that worship him must worship him in spirit and in truth.

If one is prone to splitting the hairs of the Trinity, this simply will not do. Where is the commandment to directly engage the Person of the Holy Spirit in worship? It is contained in the axiomatic logic of the Scriptures.

Acts 7:44-51
44 Our fathers had the tabernacle of witness in the wilderness [the tabernacle of Moses], *as he had appointed, speaking unto Moses, that he should make it according to the fashion that he had seen.*
45 Which also our fathers that came after brought in with Jesus [Joshua] *into the possession of the Gentiles, whom God drave out before the face of our fathers, unto the days of David;*
46 Who found favour before God, and desired to find a tabernacle [the tabernacle of David] *for the God of Jacob.*
47 But Solomon built him an house [Solomon's Temple].

48 *Howbeit the most High dwelleth not in temples* [the plural use encapsulates all the worship structures already mentioned as well as Herod's Temple that was still standing while Stephen spoke] *made with hands; as saith the prophet,*

49 *Heaven is my throne, and earth is my footstool: what house will ye build me? saith the Lord: or what is the place of my rest?*

50 *Hath not my hand made all these things?*

51 *Ye stiffnecked and uncircumcised in heart and ears, ye do always resist the Holy Ghost: as your fathers did, so do ye.*

Stephen reminded his contemporaries that though their forefathers had had the tabernacles of Moses and David and they had the temple, the most High didn't dwell in any of them. But that is exactly what they were built for, as habitations for God. Temples are built to house and honor the object of worship. Stephen declared that their lack of understanding of God's true nature—especially His omnipresence—and the fact that the temple could not contain Him amounted to resisting the Holy Spirit of God.[16] If He does not live in temples made with hands, where does He live?

1 Corinthians 3:16-17

16 *Know ye not that ye are the temple of God, and that the Spirit of God dwelleth in you?*

17 *If any man defile the temple of God, him shall God destroy; for the temple of God is holy, which temple ye are.*

1 Corinthians 6:19-20

19 *What? know ye not that your body is the temple of the Holy Ghost which is in you, which ye have of God, and ye are not your own?*

20 *For ye are bought with a price: therefore glorify God in your body, and in your spirit, which are God's.*

---

[16] This gives us some indication of how important it is to understand His true nature to be able to work with Him.

He dwells in us. We are the temple of the Holy Spirit. And temples are built to house and honor the object of worship. It stands to reason, then, that we can and should worship the Holy Spirit. If the truth that the Father, Son, and Holy Spirit are all to be worshipped causes you any consternation regarding your times of devotion (e.g., who should I pray to?), you needn't worry. When you speak to God, you speak to all Three. That is the beauty of the triune God. Worship of the entire Godhead is seen in the worship of the Name.[17] All expressions of the Godhead are found in the name of the Lord (Father) Jesus (Son) Christ (Spirit). He is "the fullness of the Godhead bodily."[18] Great indeed is the mystery of Godliness.

As we incline our hearts to worship God in spirit and in truth, He will lead us in our relationship with Him. Sometimes we need to honor the Father and feel His comforting embrace. Other times we may bow down before the Son and kiss His feet, knowing full well why they were pierced. There will be occasions when the presence of the Holy Spirit is so tangible that we cannot help but to praise Him. Worship is much more a dynamic, relational reality than it ever is an intellectual exercise. That is why intellectualism always seeks to confine worship in the corral of religious tradition and liturgy. What we cannot control generally tends to frighten us. But we need to remember that no controlling relationship is healthy.

Though the Holy Spirit rightfully receives reverence and adoration, His major role in worship is to lead us in it. In Revelation, we see Him as seven lamps before the throne of God, lighting it that we might see the object of our worship. God is Spirit, and He seeks those who will worship Him in spirit and in truth. Who better to teach us than the Holy Spirit? He fills our mouths with praise.[19] He cries out "Abba, Father" within us.[20] Spirit-led worship takes us beyond the confines of

---

[17] Ps. 8:1-2; 105:1-3; Matt. 28:19.
[18] Col. 2:9.
[19] Ps. 51:11-15.
[20] Rom. 8:15.

religious liturgy into the open pasturelands of a dynamic relationship with the Creator of the Universe.

An Operational Definition of the Trinity

I trust that all the above has helped the reader to see that the Father, the Son, and the Holy Spirit are indeed One God. This truth has been expressed theologically as the doctrine of the Trinity. That the term "Trinity" is not found in the Bible isn't sufficient reason to discard it. But if we are to use it, then it is incumbent upon us to define our terms.

The doctrine of the Trinity isn't tritheism, the idea that there are three gods of equal status in a Christian "pantheon." The doctrine of the Trinity simply stated is that:

> "In the unity of the Godhead there are Three Persons, the Father, the Son, and the Holy Spirit, these Three Persons being truly distinct from one another…In the words of the Athanasian Creed: 'the Father is God, the Son is God, and the Holy Spirit is God, and yet there are not three Gods but one God.' In this Trinity of Persons the Son is begotten of the Father by an eternal generation, and the Holy Spirit proceeds by an eternal procession from the Father and the Son. Yet, notwithstanding this difference as to origin, the Persons are co-eternal and co-equal."[21]

Now, if by co-equal we mean the continual exercise of the same authority (in level or type), we have a problem. This would confuse the different functions and aspects of the different Persons in the Godhead. On the other hand, if by co-equal we mean to say that the Three Persons of the Godhead have equally and in common with one another

---

[21] From *The Catholic Encyclopedia*, "The Blessed Trinity", http://www.knight.org/advent/cathen/15047a.htm, accessed on 6/3/1998.

the nature and perfection of supreme divinity, then the term as a theo-logical tag may be redeemed. The early church fathers invariably con-ceived each of the Three Persons as exercising distinct and separate functions.[22] Chuck Missler puts it succinctly when he says:

> "The Bible reveals to us the invisible Father, from whom all revelations proceed; the Son, who mediates and objectively incarnates that revelation as a historical reality; and the Holy Spirit, who is divinely outpoured and subjectively applies that revelation to each of us."[23]

Figure 1.2 below represents a classic graphic used to explain the Trini-ty.[24]

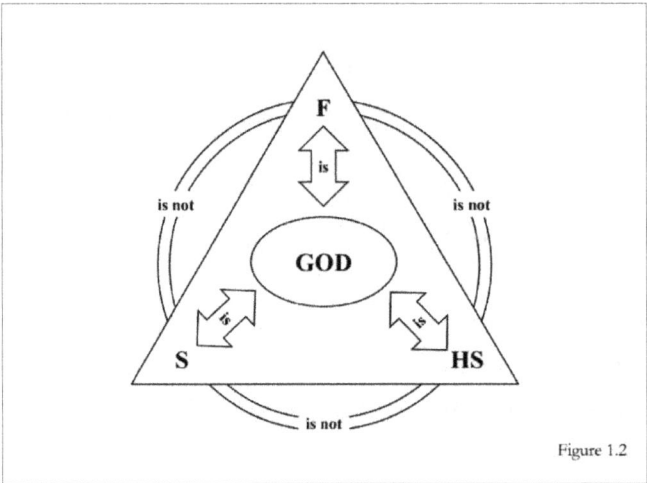

Figure 1.2

The diagram illustrates the truth that while the Father is God, the Son is God, and the Holy Spirit is God; the Father is not the Holy Spirit and the Holy Spirit is not the Son and the Son is not the Father. When I speak of the Trinity, it is with this understanding in mind, that while

---

[22] Ibid.

[23] Chuck Missler, *Personal Update – August 1995*, "One God or Three?", © 1996 by Koinonia House, Inc., P.O. Box D, Coeur d'Alene, ID 83816-0347.

[24] Adapted from H. Wayne House, *Charts of Christian Theology & Doctrine*, Zondervan Publishing House, Grand Rapids, Michigan, 1992, p. 45.

They are each God, They each play different roles in the history of our creation and redemption. For instance, the Father didn't die on the cross for you and me. The Son did. 1 Corinthians 12:4-7 is another good example of the different functions of the Persons of the Godhead.

1 Corinthians 12:4-7
4 Now there are diversities of gifts, but the same Spirit.
5 And there are differences of administrations, but the same Lord.
6 And there are diversities of operations, but it is the same God which worketh all in all.
7 But the manifestation of the Spirit is given to every man to profit withal.

The Holy Spirit dispenses the differing spiritual gifts of grace. The Son imparts the different administrations in the church. But it is the Father who is the originator and architect of the power that They—the Son and the Spirit—release in us. Each member of the Godhead plays a part for equipping us in "the manifestation of the Spirit" that is given to us all for our benefit.

The Holy Spirit is not an Impersonal Force
Charismatic[25] Christianity—that large portion of the body of Christ that believes the signs and wonders seen in the book of Acts are available to believers today—is acutely aware of the Holy Spirit's role in dispensing the gifts listed in 1 Corinthians 12:8-10.[26] In the interest of full disclosure, I must inform the reader that I am squarely within the Charismatic camp. I consider our desire and pursuit of all God has promised to the saints to be noble. But I have also noticed a tendency among us to treat the Holy Spirit more as a power source than a Person. This is seen in many of the analogies we use while instructing

---

[25] My use of "Charismatic" is general and is meant to include all those who believe in the continuance of the manifestation of the Holy Spirit in this day and age.
[26] They are: word of wisdom, word of knowledge, faith, gifts of healing, working of miracles, prophecy, discerning of spirits, diverse kinds of tongues, and the interpretation of tongues.

people in the gifts. We admonish people to "tune in" or "feel the flow" or "activate the gift." In our desire for people to experience the Holy Spirit's power, I fear we have been more concerned about effect than affect. But the latter must come before the former.

To affect means to have an effect on, to bring about a change in someone or something. We get our English word from the Latin *afficere*, "to exert influence on." From "affect" we get "affection" and "affectionate." Effect is the result of the affect. No affect, no effect. To concern ourselves with outcomes (signs, miracles, and wonders) without a solid foundation of relationship is to put the cart in front of the horse. Perhaps a story may help explain this a bit better.

Journey to Chicken Island – A Short Story
Your mother and father were proud, excited, and nervous the day you were born as most first time parents are. (If you are not a firstborn, just go with it. It is a story, after all.) As the nurse put you in the industrial bassinette to cart you off to the hospital nursery, your father patted you mother reassuringly on the shoulder. "It will be ok, honey," he said. "They'll take fine care of the baby and you can get a little rest." Your mother knew better. She tried to relax, but the uneasiness wouldn't leave her.

"Dear, take me to the baby," she said, eyes intense beneath a furrowed brow.

"Honey, they just took the boy out not an hour ago," your father protested. (If you weren't a baby boy, just go with it. Remember, it's a story.)

"I know," she said, "but I just have to see him." Against the nurse's protest, he helped your mother out of the bed and they made their way slowly to the human chicken coop.

"There he is," your father said. "Second row up, forth from the left. Isn't he precious?" She would have answered him. She would have said, "Oh, yes, dear, he's beautiful." She would have, that is, if you hadn't disappeared right then. "Oh, yes," died into a gasp that turned into a cry which grew into a howl. It wasn't the radiologist's fault. She had no way of knowing. Who could have?

As your father and mother were making their way down the hall, the radiologist two floors down was telling her patient that everything was going to be all right. The procedure wasn't dangerous at all, she said as she donned a lead jacket and stepped behind her protective wall. At the very instant that your father pointed you out by poking his finger at the glass-encased wire window, she flipped her switch and started a chain reaction that would take multiple pages to tell (complete with fancy looking physics formulas that I can't understand, let alone write) but took only a nanosecond to complete. The power surge from the nearby electrical substation combined with the super-charged x-ray quantum gun and broke loose through faulty wiring in the hospital to connect with the DNA signature in your father's finger and opened up a worm hole in your bassinette, which swallowed you whole. (I know, I know. Far-fetched. But if you saw those fancy formulas, you might believe me.)

Your mother's screaming was understandable. But she may have been comforted to know that you landed on a lush island inhabited by goat-milking chickens. These chickens made sure that you had enough milk to drink and they protected you from the elements and hid you from predators. And you grew.

One day while you were chasing the goats with the chickens to get a glass of milk, you noticed an odd looking creature walking toward you on the beach. Then it dawned on you. It is another human walking to-ward you. "Nikolas," you cry out, recognizing me from my back cover photo on this book, "how did you ever find me?"

31

"Never mind that now," I said, tugging at my shirtsleeve to cover up my embarrassing x-ray burn. "Your father is coming and I have to prepare you for what to expect." We spend the next several hours together as I teach you how a hug feels, what happens to your hair when your head is kissed as compared to when it's patted, the heat your posterior may feel as the result of a swat, and the exhilarating feeling of being thrown in the air and caught again.

As our little seminar draws to a close, a man walks up to us from the shore. The chickens part before him as he nears you. With tears in his eyes, he embraces you. You feel the constriction of your arms, the warmth of his chest, the greater difficulty in breathing that somehow is more comforting than disconcerting and recognize that you are being hugged just as I had described it to you. "Throw me in the air," you shout, "I want to experience all my father can do." Your father obliges. He tosses you in the air and joyfully catches you before you hit the sand. What a rush! Your father's powerful arms propel you beyond your own ability to break with gravity and catch you before you crash under gravity's renewed grip. You know excitement. You know the sensation of a comforting hug. You have experienced the power of limited flight. What you don't know is why your father is doing all these things. You haven't been taught that his hug is an exhibition of his longing for you, his swat a reminder of his love, his toss an expression of his joy. You recognize the effects of being around him but not the affection they communicate. Imagine your father's heartbreak when he realizes that you are coming to him just for recreation and not relationship.

Return from Chicken Island – Back to Reality
The Holy Spirit is not an impersonal force. He is a Person. As a person, He has the same attributes that mark you as a person. He has thoughts, a will, memories[27], and emotions. Like you, He is self-aware.

---

[27] John 14:26.

1 Corinthians 2:10-11

10 But God hath revealed them unto us by his Spirit: for the Spirit searcheth all things, yea, the deep things of God.

11 For what man knoweth the things of a man, save the spirit of man which is in him? even so the things of God knoweth no man, but the Spirit of God.

What makes you self-aware? What is the entity that monitors your thoughts? How are you able to talk to yourself? The spirit of man within you is the core of your being. It is the heart of who you are. Would you be willing to simply call that a "life force" and regard it as a non-sentient part of your being? I didn't think so. But in many practical ways, we are willing to do just that with the Holy Spirit. It is the Spirit that knows the things of God even as it is the spirit of man that knows the things of man. The Holy Spirit is not only Self-aware; He plumbs the depth of the heart, will, and emotions of the Father and the Son. Talk about relationship!

The Holy Spirit's Marks of Personhood
If I stick my finger into an electrical outlet, I am sure to have a memorable experience. The encounter will undoubtedly modify my future behavior toward all things electric. But the outlet itself is nothing to me but the source of the experience. I won't try to talk to it, hang out with it, or even look longingly at it. I may read about electrical outlets to figure out how best to receive benefit from it and avoid being burned. But even this exercise falls far short of fellowship. And if I began evidencing undue fondness for inanimate wiring, you would rightly judge me odd. But somehow, when we treat the Person of the Holy Spirit as an impersonal force it doesn't cause us heart burn.

Getting to know a person requires more than just shaking their hand. Conversation and openness over time develops the bonds of friendship. It is in those encounters that we learn what a person knows, wants, and feels. Along with self-awareness, the Holy Spirit bears these other marks of personhood. He has knowledge, a will, and emotions.

Isaiah 11:2
And the spirit of the Lord shall rest upon him, the spirit of wisdom and understanding, the spirit of counsel and might, the spirit of knowledge and of the fear of the Lord;

He is not the Spirit of data storage. He is the Spirit of knowledge, and knowledge connotes awareness and experience.

1 Corinthians 12:11
But all these worketh that one and the selfsame Spirit, dividing to every man severally as he will.

The Holy Spirit distributes gifts in accordance to His own will. As Jesus subjugated His will to the Father,[28] so the Spirit subjects Himself to Jesus Christ.[29] And the Father Himself submits to the requests of the Holy Spirit.[30] This does not indicate any greater authority on one part of the Godhead over the other. It simply illustrates the principle of submission. Submitting doesn't indicate a lack of will. Quite to the contrary, one must have a will to submit. The Godhead models this for us perfectly. Because of submission, They can work in perfect unity without any jealousy of position.[31]

Acts 13:2-4
2 As they ministered to the Lord and fasted, the Holy Spirit said, "Now separate to Me Barnabas and Saul for the work to which I have called them."

---

[28] John 5:30; Matt. 26:39.
[29] John 16:13-15.
[30] Rom. 8:26-27. Also, Jesus was led of the Spirit (Matt. 4:1) and the Spirit was directed by Jesus (John 16:7; Acts 2:32-33).
[31] Phil. 2:5-11.

3 Then, having fasted and prayed, and laid hands on them, they sent them away.

4 So, being sent out by the Holy Spirit, they went down to Seleucia, and from there they sailed to Cyprus. NKJV

Could you imagine the reaction this would have caused if we were talking about a human governing body? Suppose a dedicated group of Marines gathered to honor their commanding general. Right in the middle of the ceremonies, while the gunnery sergeant was praising the general for his vast accomplishments and strategic acumen, another general crashes the party and says, "Jones and Franklin, front and center. I am sending you off on a special mission. You leave tomorrow." Jones and Franklin might not say anything but "Yes, sir!" The commanding general, on the other hand, may have ideas of his own regarding Jones and Franklin. And who was this other general to come in and crash his party?

Not so the Godhead. The church in Antioch is deeply absorbed in a dedicated worship time of ministering to the Lord Jesus. In the middle of the festivities, the Holy Spirit calls out Barnabas and Saul and gives them marching orders. The King of kings isn't put off one bit. He was probably smiling as the Holy Spirit went to work. After all, it's Jesus' orders that He communicates. But note how He personalizes it. "Now separate **to Me** Barnabas and Saul for the work to which **I have called them**." With such ownership over direction, how could we ever doubt that the Holy Spirit has a will?

Ephesians 4:30
And grieve not the holy Spirit of God, whereby ye are sealed unto the day of redemption.

The Holy Spirit has emotions. He can be grieved. Let me ask you, have you ever seen your electrical outlet shed tears of sorrow? Do you know why the Holy Spirit grieves? Because He loves.[32] And as any ardent lover worth his salt, He feels great longing and jealousy.[33] And these are not His only emotions. Remember the fruit of the Spirit?

Galatians 5:22-23
22 But the fruit of the Spirit is love, joy, peace, longsuffering, gentleness, goodness, faith,
23 Meekness, temperance: against such there is no law.

It is His fruit. The reason He can cause us to bear them is because they express His nature: love, joy, peace, longsuffering, gentleness, goodness. These all have emotional qualities. And it is His emotion—His passion—that brings richness and depth to the relationship.

Yes, the Holy Spirit is God. He is a Person. And as a Person, He desires fellowship with us. He was the one who moved holy men of God to write about Him using symbolic language that we might know how to keep in step with Him.[34] Let's dive in, shall we?

---

[32] Rom. 5:5; 15:30.
[33] James 4:5.
[34] Gal. 5:25 NIV.

CHAPTER 2

Wind
The breath of God in us

I said, "Let's dive in," but I think we should go sailing first. Nothing in life quite compares to cutting through the water on a sailboat. The crude belching of an internal combustion engine is thankfully absent. Only the elegant sounds of slapping waves and snapping fabric caress your ears as you fly with the wind. Exhilarating! And why shouldn't it be? The wind is one of the most powerful things experienced by mankind, or the universe, for that matter.

Genesis 1:1-2
1 In the beginning God created the Heaven and the earth.
2 And the earth was without form, and void; and darkness was upon
the face of the deep. And the Spirit of God moved upon the face of
the waters.

Three prominent symbols for the Holy Spirit make their appearance in verse two. But wind is mentioned first, so we will begin there. The Hebrew word translated "Spirit" in verse two is *ruwach*, which means "wind." This symbol is actually part of His name: the Holy Wind. In referring to Himself in this way, He has given us a great insight into His nature.

What Is Wind?

Simply stated, wind is air in motion.[35] But you knew I couldn't leave it at that, didn't you? To get the full benefit from this symbol, we not only need to know what wind is, but also how it develops and what interacts and interferes with it.

Let's go back to the beginning—Genesis 1. Here we have a description of the earth as "formless and void" and the Spirit of God moving across the face of the deep. He fluttered over the universe as an eagle flutters over her nest.[36] We are asked to envision the Wind of God hovering over all that there was in the universe. In other words, He is omnipresent. God then calls light into being and subsequently divides the waters with a firmament He calls heaven. This macrocosmic event is repeated every day on a microscopic scale in a process we call the Hydrologic Cycle. When water is heated, it evaporates and rises. As it rises, it cools, condenses, and falls. This simple picture of moving water is the same process that causes wind.

Imagine the earth as smooth and motionless. The heat of the Sun would fall most directly on the equator. Air there would warm and rise, causing a low pressure at the earth's surface and a high pressure in the upper atmosphere. Because air at the poles is colder and of a higher pressure, it would move to fill the void. Thus, on the surface of the earth the air would move from the poles to the equator. But in the upper atmosphere, it would move from the equator to the poles. This happens because a high pressure at the surface means a low pressure in the upper atmosphere and vice versa. The Figure 2.1 below illustrates this simple model.[37]

---

[35] Motion is a common quality in all the symbols used for the Holy Spirit. Living water, anointing oil, flaming fire, a column of cloud, descending doves; these all move.

[36] In Deut. 32:11 "fluttereth" is translated from the same Hebrew word as "moved" in Gen. 1:2. The word is *rachaph*.

[37] Adapted from Pidwirny, M., *Fundamentals of Physical Geography (2nd Edition)*, © 1999-2008 Michael Pidwirny, accessed 5/14/2008, http://www.physicalgeography.net/fundamentals/7p.html.

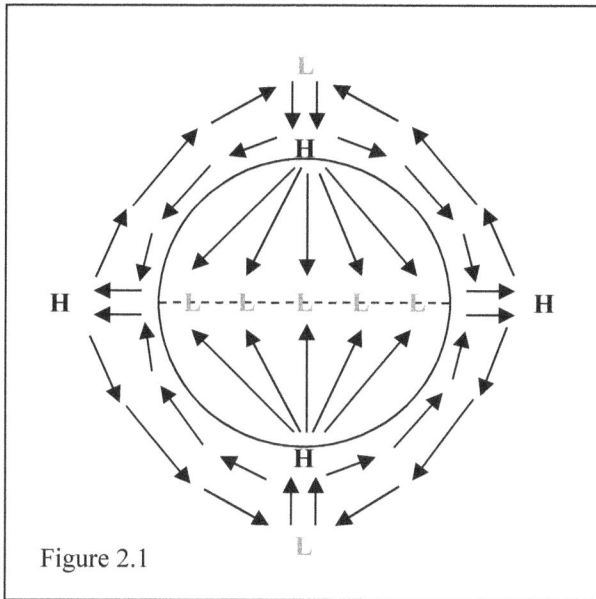

Figure 2.1

I trust you feel a sense of motion as you look at this diagram. Even in a simple model, pervasive winds would permeate the earth. But they would do so in a rather predictable fashion. South of the equator, wind would blow north. And north of the equator, the wind would blow south. But once we add the earth's spin, a picture closer to what we actually experience emerges.[38]

---
[38] Ibid.

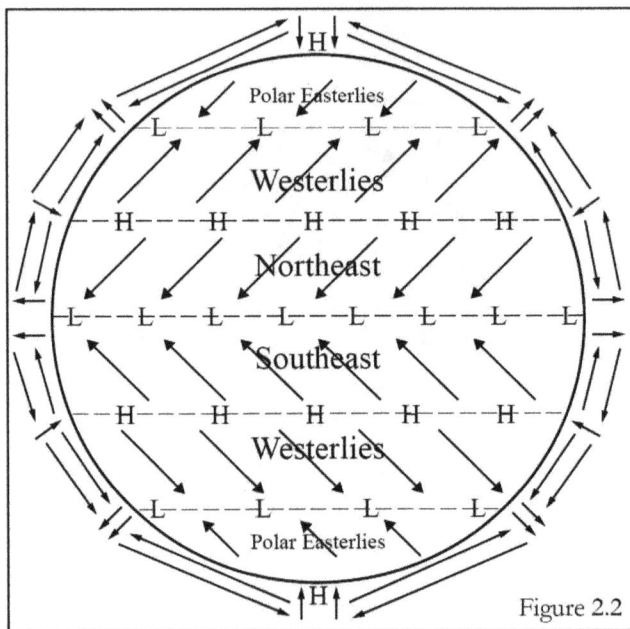

Figure 2.2

Of course, the surface of the earth isn't uniform. Not only do land and water absorb the heat of the sun at different rates, the land itself is uneven. Uneven heat distribution, differing topography, and competing winds all interfere with prevailing wind patterns. It is because of this complexity that so many people make a living trying to predict what the wind will do. Let's look at one more simple wind model and then we will begin to apply our observations.

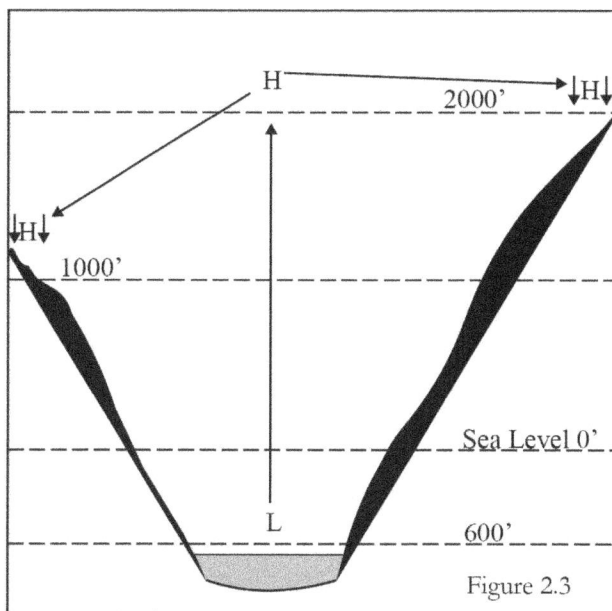

Figure 2.3

Figure 2.3 is an illustration of typical wind currents over the Sea of Galilee (particularly at night). The water's surface is roughly 685 feet below sea level. The land on the western coast of the lake rises to 1,000 feet above sea level and to the east it is as high as 2,000 feet. This topography makes the Sea of Galilee susceptible to sudden and violent wind storms. These winds can churn up great waves because the water is only 200 feet deep and is less able to absorb the wind's energy than a deeper body of water could. These were the types of storms that Jesus and His disciples faced while ministering in the Galilee.

How Is the Wind Like the Holy Spirit?

We have already pointed out that wind is universal. The gases around us that compose the atmosphere are in constant motion. There are times, it is true, that the air mass about us is still—but it is never technically motionless. As the atmosphere mantles the earth and its breath is felt in every place, so the Holy Spirit is everywhere breathing life and direction wherever He wills.

Wind is irresistible. You can hide from it, block it, or try to avoid it. But you can't stop it. As Jesus told Nicodemus, "The wind blows wherever it pleases."[39] In like manner, the Spirit of God moves where He pleases. People can try to avoid Him and even resist Him, but they can't stop Him. He will accomplish what He sets out to do. Strong winds teach us of His power. Gentle breezes remind us of His loving kindness. Resisting the Spirit can derail your life. But if you let His wind fill your sails, you will go far.

Wind is invisible. We can see its effects. But we can't see it. God is also invisible.[40] It is on the basis of His invisibility that He shows Himself greater than the creation and prohibits us from making any graven images to worship.[41] Though the Godhead has and does show Himself in physical form, their true nature is superluminal—faster than light. They are beyond visual perception. Imagine if they weren't. Since God is omnipresent, if He were visible we would be unable to see anything else. Aren't you glad that God in His wisdom made air transparent?

Wind is universal and intimate. "Let everything that has breath praise the Lord," the psalmist sang.[42] Our breath is a personal wind that proves we are alive. In like manner, the Holy Spirit is all around us, but also in us.[43] At the risk of mixing metaphors, the wind and our breath are an illustration of the anointing *upon* the believer and the anointing *within* the believer. Comparing wind and breath can also help us gain some perspective on the Spirit's supply relative to our need. The volume of Earth's atmosphere is approximately 17.25×10^{21} liters. Think of that as 17,250,000,000,000,000,000,000 liters of available air to fill our lungs that can at maximum only hold 6 liters. If this

---

[39] John 3:8a NIV.
[40] Rom. 1:20; 1 Tim. 1:17; Col 1:15.
[41] Deut. 4:15-19.
[42] Ps. 150:6.
[43] John 14:17.

fact from the natural realm boggles the mind, think for a moment about the limitless Holy Spirit who lives inside you.

Air moves into warm places. Earth is windy because the sun is hot. As the air heats, it rises causing a low pressure. God wants us to be on fire for Him. A church that basks in the warmth of His love[44] will move out in ministry and outreach. A hot church is a "going" church, a "sending" church. Subsequently, its population density decreases—creating a spiritual low pressure, making room for others to come in. And like the Hydrologic Cycle, the process repeats itself.

The wind can be captured, but it can't be controlled. Sailors tack with their sails to catch the wind and ride through the waves. But they can't control the wind direction. Their progress across the sea is dependent on their cooperation with the wind. So it is with us. In our journey to the heart of God, we certainly can't control Him or the messages He sends us. But if we cooperate with His direction, we will find ourselves coming ashore to our true home.

Friction with the earth slows wind down. If we give leeway to our flesh—the dust of the earth—we will cause friction with the work of the Holy Spirit in our lives. Our growth and progress in the kingdom will slow down. Our flesh is what the serpent feeds on.[45] It is also the part of us that resists the Spirit most strongly.

Galatians 5:17
For the flesh lusteth against the Spirit, and the Spirit against the flesh: and these are contrary the one to the other: so that ye cannot do the things that ye would.

Following the Spirit is the only way to avoid falling in lust with the flesh. Sailboats don't work well on land.

---

[44] Rom. 5:5.

[45] Gen. 3:14 Our flesh was made of the dust of the earth and dust is what the serpent was cursed to eat.

Jesus and the Wind

The apostle John wrote one of the most profound personal encounters recorded in Scripture. Nicodemus, a Pharisee and member of the Sanhedrin, came to Jesus under the cover of darkness to sound Him out. The poor man had no idea how deep the well went. It is through this conversation that we learn about being "born again." John 3:16, a verse used to evangelize the world, was spoken by Jesus to Nicodemus alone. Yes, Jesus taught the multitudes. We know He instructed His disciples. But this record shows us the mastery of the Teacher as He ministers to one man.

John 3:6-8
6 That which is born of the flesh is flesh; and that which is born of the Spirit is spirit.
7 Marvel not that I said unto thee, Ye must be born again.
8 The wind bloweth where it listeth, and thou hearest the sound thereof, but canst not tell whence it cometh, and whither it goeth: so is every one that is born of the Spirit.

That which is born of the Spirit is spirit. If those born of the Spirit are like the wind, it stands to reason that the Spirit is also. This is even more apparent in the Greek, for the term translated "wind" and "Spirit" in verse 8 is the same word: *pneuma*. In gaining an understanding of the wind, we not only get insights into the Spirit of God, we also begin to understand ourselves and how people react to us.

When a breeze comes over us, we might be able to tell its general direction. But its point of origin and final destination are a mystery. Those who are led of the Spirit appear the same way to natural man. The unregenerate cannot tell where we are coming from nor understand where we are going. It is foolishness to them. But as we blow by, there are those who will catch the irresistible fresh scent of the Spirit and want to know more.

John 8:14, 21-22

14 Jesus answered and said unto them, Though I bear record of myself, yet my record is true: for I know whence I came, and whither I go; but ye cannot tell whence I come, and whither I go.

21 Then said Jesus again unto them, I go my way, and ye shall seek me, and shall die in your sins: whither I go, ye cannot come.

22 Then said the Jews, Will he kill himself? because he saith, Whither I go, ye cannot come.

When Jesus spoke to the unbelieving multitude about His origin and final destination, they took it for a suicide note. They couldn't have been farther off the mark if they had tried. As one "born of the Spirit"[46], He was a wind they couldn't understand. But as He continued to preach, many believed on Him.[47]

Luke 8:22-25

22 Now it came to pass on a certain day, that he went into a ship with his disciples: and he said unto them, Let us go over unto the other side of the lake. And they launched forth.

23 But as they sailed he fell asleep: and there came down a storm of wind on the lake; and they were filled with water, and were in jeopardy.

24 And they came to him, and awoke him, saying, Master, master, we perish. Then he arose, and rebuked the wind and the raging of the water: and they ceased, and there was a calm.

25 And he said unto them, Where is your faith? And they being afraid wondered, saying one to another, What manner of man is this! for he commandeth even the winds and water, and they obey him.

The wind in these verses is not *pneuma* but *anemos*, which means "a current of air." It is the most common New Testament term translated "wind." Aside from its literal meaning, it also refers to "the four winds

---

46 Luke 1:35.
47 John 8:29-30.

of the earth"[48] that do the Lord's bidding. We will speak of these shortly. It is also used metaphorically of false teachings that deceive and drive apart the body of Christ.[49]

As Figures 2.2 and 2.3 illustrate, another factor that affects wind speed and current are competing or combating air flows. When different air fronts collide, storms often happen. Look at Figure 2.3 and imagine the winds screaming down to the middle of the lake and churning up waves large enough to swamp your boat. Then imagine Jesus calmly sleeping in the storm.

The wind of the Spirit on this occasion was the command of Jesus, "Let us go over to the other side of the lake." This was the word of the Lord. So the storm that came down upon them was a combating and conflicting wind. It was not in the will of the Lord. He rebuked the wind and the waves for coming against Him and then rebuked the disciples for not having faith in His word. Had I been in the boat with Him, no doubt my jaw would have dropped in amazement with all the disciples. Water to wine is one thing, but here was a man who could command the wind and the sea. And what did they encounter on the other side of the lake?

Luke 8:26-29
26 And they arrived at the country of the Gadarenes, which is over against Galilee.
27 And when he went forth to land, there met him out of the city a certain man, which had devils long time, and ware no clothes, neither abode in any house, but in the tombs.
28 When he saw Jesus, he cried out, and fell down before him, and with a loud voice said, What have I to do with thee, Jesus, thou Son of God most high? I beseech thee, torment me not.
*29 (For he had commanded the **unclean spirit** [pneuma] to come out of the man. For oftentimes it had caught him: and he was kept*

---

[48] Rev. 7:1.
[49] Eph. 4:14; Jude 12.

bound with chains and in fetters; and he brake the bands, and was driven of the devil into the wilderness.) [Emphasis added.]

Unclean or evil spirits are opposing wind forces to the Holy Spirit. Just as Jesus rebuked the wind, He also commanded evil spirits out of people. Wind resistance in our lives doesn't just come from the flesh. We are embroiled in a spiritual battle. When winds of opposition blow on us, we should not be afraid of the storm. We should rebuke the wind.

Messages in the Wind
Psalm 148:7-8
7 Praise the LORD from the earth, you great sea creatures and all ocean depths,
*8 lightning and hail, snow and clouds, **stormy winds that do his bidding**,* [Emphasis added.] *NIV*

As He proved from the swamped stern of the disciples' ship, the stormy winds do His bidding indeed. Wind is part of the creation, and as such, it must obey its Creator.

Psalm 104:4
He makes winds his messengers, *flames of fire his servants.* [Emphasis added.] *NIV*

Strictly interpreted, Psalm 104:4 is talking about angels. And Deuteronomy 25:4 is talking about oxen, but Paul applies it to ministers.[50] So please bear with me a little in my folly as I apply this verse to spatial differences in atmospheric pressures: "He makes winds his messengers." Did you know that God says something different with an east wind than He does with a west wind? The wind speaks, and He expects His people to understand the prophetic import of the weather.

---

[50] 1 Cor. 9:6-10.

Luke 12:54-56

54 And he said also to the people, When ye see a cloud rise out of the west, straightway ye say, There cometh a shower; and so it is.

55 And when ye see the south wind blow, ye say, There will be heat; and it cometh to pass.

56 Ye hypocrites, ye can discern the face of the sky and of the earth; but how is it that ye do not discern this time?

As Romans 1:20 states, the visible creation instructs us about the invisible power of the Godhead. Jesus chided His contemporaries because they could discern the impact of a prevailing wind but were insensitive to the prophetic warning of the times they were living in. In fact, He did worse than chide. He called them hypocrites. He considered it hypocritical on their part to forecast the weather and yet not be able to discern the time they were living in. What about us?

Back in the days when we had cable television, my wife's favorite channel was The Weather Channel. She is still fascinated with the weather and does a good job staying abreast of what is coming our way. I must confess, I am a bit oblivious to weather predictions or conditions. I usually find out what it is when I walk outside, unless my wife has already warned me. Just the other day, she called me on my cell phone while I was driving to work to let me know that they had issued a tornado warning near our area. As someone who grew up in Tornado Alley, you would think I would pay more attention to such things! There is something else about my wife I must confess. She is more prophetic than I am and often several years ahead of me regarding what is coming our way. Coincidence? I think not. She isn't hypocritical. She can discern both the wind of the weather *and* the wind of the Spirit.

The Lord expects us to know the Spirit's wind direction. Several years ago, I was part of a team ministering at a pastors' conference in Romania. During one of the sessions, the pastor leading our team invited the conference attendees to come up for prophetic ministry. I was in the front row of the congregation facing him as he laid hands on people and spoke over them. I noticed something odd as I interceded for him. I was speaking the prophecies he was speaking, only I was doing so a fraction of a second ahead of him. This became rather distracting to my intercessory efforts. It took me a minute to realize that the Spirit was blowing through the church from the back to the front. Because of where I was positioned, I was catching the breeze of prophecy an instant before he was. Well, my assignment that night wasn't to prophesy, it was to pray! I dove off the front row and tucked myself behind him between the stage and the piano. Out of the direct impact of the Wind, I was much better able to hold him up in prayer.

Knowing wind direction is not only important for the fulfilling of your mission, it can be a message in and of itself. Modern meteorology classifies winds using sixteen principal compass bearings. Thankfully, God has kept it simple for us. He has four.

Ezekiel 37:9
Then said he unto me, Prophesy unto the wind, prophesy, son of man, and say to the wind, Thus saith the Lord God; Come from **the four winds**, *O breath, and breathe upon these slain, that they may live.* [Emphasis added.]

As you might guess, these winds bear the names of the principal compass directions: east, west, south, and north. The convention is to name the wind according to the direction it is blowing *from*. Each of these winds brought distinct weather patterns to the land of Israel. The impact these prevailing winds had on the land was used by God as powerful illustrations of what He was doing through the Spirit. Judgment, deliverance, war, and the presence of God all blow in on the wings of the wind.

The East Wind of Judgment

Jeremiah 18:17
I will scatter them as with an east wind before the enemy; I will shew them the back, and not the face, in the day of their calamity.

The east wind comes out of the Arabian Desert as a hot, scorching blast that withers the leaves of plants and the souls of men. It is a wind of judgment.

Hosea 13:15
Though he be fruitful among his brethren, an east wind shall come, the wind of the Lord shall come up from the wilderness [NIV – the desert], *and his spring shall become dry, and his fountain shall be dried up: he shall spoil the treasure of all pleasant vessels.*

The east wind scatters and scorches in judgment. Jesus said that when the Holy Spirit came, He would convict the world of sin, righteousness, and judgment.[51] His judgment blows in from the east.

Jeremiah 4:11-12
11 At that time it will be said to this people and to Jerusalem, A hot wind from the bare heights in the wilderness {comes at My command} against the daughter of My people — not {a wind} to fan or cleanse {from chaff, as when threshing, but}
12 A wind too strong and full for winnowing comes at My word. Now I will also speak in judgment against {My people}. AMP

"The bare heights in the wilderness" are to the east of Israel. It is thus the east wind that Jeremiah speaks of. The east wind is too strong for winnowing. It blows everything away.

The West Wind of Winnowing

Do you recall what John the Baptist said about the winnowing wind?

---

[51] John 16:8.

Matthew 3:11-12

11 I indeed baptize you with water unto repentance: but he that cometh after me is mightier than I, whose shoes I am not worthy to bear: he shall baptize you with the Holy Ghost, and with fire:

12 Whose fan is in his hand, and he will throughly purge his floor, and gather his wheat into the garner; but he will burn up the chaff with unquenchable fire.

Winnowing is the process of tossing threshed wheat up into the air with a pitchfork to allow the wind to catch the chaff and blow it away while the grain falls to the ground. This was usually done in the late afternoon with the aid of the prevailing westerly winds. Think of the imagery that John the Baptist is using: a man with a pitchfork tending a fire. The devil hijacked this picture in a red leotard with a pointy tail. Fire isn't the devil's friend, it is his undoing.[52] But I get ahead of myself. We'll save the rest of the fireside chat for Chapter 4.

A winnowing wind is a good thing. It removes the chaff and leaves the fruit. It is a purging, cleansing wind. But if we determine to cling to those things that the Lord would see us freed from, He will only blow harder.

Jeremiah 4:13

Behold, he shall come up as clouds, and his chariots shall be as a whirlwind: his horses are swifter than eagles. Woe unto us! for we are spoiled.

The wind intended to set us free, if ignored, can become a gale that ruins us. If we are deaf to the Spirit's conviction of sin and righteousness, judgment is sure to follow. As Paul instructed the Corinthian church, we should judge ourselves to avoid being judged. His leading of us in the winnowing wind is always gentler than His chastising hand. But even when He does chastise, He does so out of love to set us

---

[52] Rev. 20:10.

free.[53] What are we to do when we find ourselves in a windstorm of judgment? Repent!

Jeremiah 4:14
O Jerusalem, wash thine heart from wickedness, that thou mayest be saved. How long shall thy vain thoughts lodge within thee?

We need to let the Lord's winnowing fork into our hearts so He can lift out our fruitless imaginings and ungodly beliefs to the cleansing breeze of the Spirit. But if we resist the Holy Spirit of God, the wind speed is bound to pick up and can threaten to blow us away like a scorching east wind. What are we to do? We need to stop harboring wicked thoughts and let them go. We need to be washed in the blood of Jesus. He will surely then command the wind to calm down.

The West Wind of Deliverance
We've already seen the west wind winnowing its way through the wheat. It works to set us free of the chaff in our lives. This chaff is not only worthless thoughts—idols of the mind—but also the enemies that oppose us.

Psalms 35:4-5
4 Let them be confounded and put to shame that seek after my soul: let them be turned back and brought to confusion that devise my hurt.
5 Let them be as chaff before the wind: and let the angel of the Lord chase them.

We don't wrestle against flesh and blood, but against spiritual wickedness.[54] When we allow the winnowing wind to blow through us, it removes those things that might give the devil claim in us. Jesus said, "The ruler of this world is coming, and he has nothing in Me."[55] Satan couldn't touch Jesus because Jesus had nothing in Himself that be-

---

[53] 1 Cor. 11:31-32.
[54] Eph. 6:12.
[55] John 14:30 NKJV.

longed to the devil. The devil had no claim on Him. Jesus's journey to and through the cross was entirely at His discretion, not the devil's. He wants to make us untouchable too. The more chaff He blows out, the less the devil can reach in. And if we become truly transparent, the Wind can blow right through us to chase the enemy away. Let's backtrack to the east wind for a moment:

Exodus 10:13
And Moses stretched forth his rod over the land of Egypt, and the Lord brought an east wind upon the land all that day, and all that night; and when it was morning, the east wind brought the locusts.

Remember, the east wind brings judgment. In this case, it brought the plague of locusts. Locusts in Scripture represent the destructive powers of the enemy. In Revelation 9, the destroying spirit army that arises like smoke out of the bottomless pit is pictured as a fantastic locust swarm led by Apollyon, the Destroyer. The locusts brought to Egypt on the east wind destroyed every green herb and tree. Seeing the devastation, Pharaoh confessed his sin and asked for forgiveness. How did the Lord respond to his repentance?

Exodus 10:19
And the Lord turned a mighty strong west wind, which took away the locusts, and cast them into the Red sea; there remained not one locust in all the coasts of Egypt.

It is the west wind that drives plagues away. What had been plaguing the Israelites for centuries? Their Egyptian taskmasters. At the edge of the Red Sea, Moses lifted his staff with arms stretched high. Wind from the east rushed in at the Lord's command and blew hard all night. In the morning, the children of Israel journeyed across the Red Sea on a dry ground. But when the Egyptians gave chase, the wind that held the waters up like a wall turned back on itself to make the waves crash down on them all. The horse and rider were cast into the sea by the breath of YHWH, the Man of War.[56]

The South Winds of War
Habakkuk 3:3, 13

3 God came from Teman [Heb., the south], *and the Holy One from mount Paran. Selah. His glory covered the heavens, and the earth was full of his praise.*

13 Thou wentest forth for the salvation of thy people, even for salvation with thine anointed; thou woundedst the head out of the house of the wicked, by discovering the foundation unto the neck. Selah.

The Lord approaches from the south with warfare on His mind. He comes out of the south to save His people and cleave the head of the wicked open—down to the neck. As Moses declared, the Lord is a man of war. He does not shy away from bloody battle. Isaiah prophetically pictures Him approaching Jerusalem from Edom in the south, His garments already stained and spattered with the blood of the vanquished. With fire in His eyes, He rides north to deliver His people.[57]

Zechariah 9:13-16

13 When I have bent Judah for me, filled the bow with Ephraim, and raised up thy sons, O Zion, against thy sons, O Greece, and made thee as the sword of a mighty man.

*14 And the Lord shall be seen over them, and his arrow shall go forth as the lightning: and the Lord God shall blow the trumpet, and shall go with **whirlwinds of the south**.* [Emphasis added]

15 The Lord of hosts shall defend them; and they shall devour, and subdue with sling stones; and they shall drink, and make a noise as through wine; and they shall be filled like bowls, and as the corners of the altar.

---

[56] Ex. 14:21-22; 15:9-10.
[57] Isa. 63:1-6, Rev. 19:11-15.

16 And the Lord their God shall save them in that day as the flock of his people: for they shall be as the stones of a crown, lifted up as an ensign upon his land.

We are citizens of Zion and as such we are called upon to stand against the spirit of Greece. What is the spirit of Greece? Individualistic, democratic, enlightened rationalism; otherwise known as Western culture. On the surface, this doesn't sound too bad. In a redeemed state, Western culture has done much to bring freedom and innovation to mankind and has facilitated the spread of the Gospel over the globe. But without redemption, without the opposition of the sons of Zion, Western culture has also given us the two bloodiest wars in the history of man and a modern mentality that bows down to the twin altars of relativistic morality and perverted tolerance. The Spirit of God is at war with these idols of unrighteousness.

Zechariah 4:6
Then he answered and spake unto me, saying, This is the word of the Lord unto Zerubbabel, saying, Not by might, nor by power, but by my spirit, saith the Lord of hosts.

In this battle, we must war in the Spirit. In the tabernacle of Moses, the lampstand lit the holy place for the ministering priests. This lampstand represented the Holy Spirit. We will examine its significance in detail in Chapter 6. But for now, it will suffice to take notice of where it was situated.

Exodus 26:35
Place the table outside the curtain on the north side of the tabernacle and put the lampstand opposite it on the south side. NIV

In the Song of Solomon, the Bridegroom describes His beloved as garden locked up and a spring that is sealed.[58] She in turn cries to the wind to release her fragrance abroad that her Beloved may feast.

Song of Solomon 4:16
Awake, O north wind; and come, thou south; blow upon my garden, that the spices thereof may flow out. Let my beloved come into his garden, and eat his pleasant fruits.

The hot south winds of war mixed with the cool north wind of renewal work together to release the Bride's fragrance beyond her four walls.[59]

The North Wind of God's Presence
The north wind brings the presence of God. The first chapter of Ezekiel gives us perhaps the most dramatic example of this when the prophet looks up and sees the chariot of God, the whirlwind, coming out of the north.[60] Job gives us a taste of this as well.

Job 37:21-22
21 Even now men cannot look at the light when it is bright in the skies, When the wind has passed and cleared them.
22 He comes from the north as golden splendor; With God is awesome majesty. NKJV

There are times that the Holy Spirit moves among us with the palpable presence of the Almighty. His clearing wind removes all obstructions to the Light, dispelling darkness and shadow from our midst. They are times to be truly savored.

Setting Our Sails to Catch the Wind
Extreme calm is burdensome and depressing. Near the equator there are regions of great calm and little wind that sailors called "the dol-

---

[58] Song of Sol. 4:8-15.
[59] 2 Cor. 2:14-17.
[60] See Chapter 9 for a more detailed discussion of this account.

drums." Imagine yourself a seaman in the heyday of wind power stalled on the endless ocean for days on end with stale air and sad sagging sails. The sea is a glassy mirror, the sky bright and bare of clouds. You swab the clean deck again and again, feeling no wind to pull your ropes homeward bound to family and friends. Little wonder sailors used a term synonymous with depression to describe these seas. We've all had seasons in life when, for whatever reason, we have found ourselves in the doldrums. Our progress has been halted. Our tasks are all busywork. Life about us seems stagnant and heavy. We need the Wind. How do we catch it? With the four Rs: repent, receive, Rock, and rudder.

Acts 3:19
Repent *ye therefore, and be converted, that your sins may be blotted out, when the times of refreshing shall come from the presence of the Lord;*

This "refreshing" in the Greek literally means "to recover one's breath." It is to breathe again. This power comes "from the presence of the Lord." Whenever we repent, Jesus sends us a fresh breeze of Holy Spirit to revive us.

John 20:21-22
21 Then said Jesus to them again, Peace be unto you: as my Father hath sent me, even so send I you.
*22 And when he had said this, he breathed on them, and saith unto them, **Receive** ye the Holy Ghost: KJV*

The Greek word translated "receive" in verse 22 is *lambano*, which means to take with the hand. It is more of an active grabbing than it is the passive reception of an open palm awaiting alms. We see the type of action Jesus means by the use of the same word in the book of Revelation.

Revelation 5:6-7

6 And I beheld, and, lo, in the midst of the throne and of the four beasts, and in the midst of the elders, stood a Lamb as it had been slain, having seven horns and seven eyes, which are the seven Spirits of God sent forth into all the earth.

*7 And he came and **took** [lambano] the book out of the right hand of him that sat upon the throne. KJV*

When the refreshing wind of the Holy Spirit comes in response to our repentance, we need to actively grab hold of what He brings us. We need to embrace His renewing forgiveness and let Him work in us.

Matthew 7:24-25

*24 Therefore whosoever heareth these sayings of mine, and doeth them, I will liken him unto a wise man, which built his house upon a **rock**:*

*25 And the rain descended, and the floods came, and the winds blew, and beat upon that house; and it fell not: for it was founded upon a **rock**. KJV*

Following what Jesus says—doing it—is being a disciple. This is building our house upon the Rock. This parable is often applied to the storms in life that can cause catastrophic failures of faith in those who don't establish their walk on actual obedience to Jesus, people who gladly listen but fail to do. I find no fault with this view. I simply want to amplify it a bit.

Rains, floods, and winds are also emblematic in Scripture of moves of the Holy Spirit. Have you ever fallen apart in the presence of God? There are many in the body of Christ who criticize the Pentecostal expression of faith due to the excesses they see in Charismatic services. Shaking, rolling, uncontrollable laughter or weeping, and falling out are viewed as hyper-emotionalism at best or demonization at worst. Many Pentecostals use the term "slain in the Spirit" without much thought to the contradictory ideals contained in the idiom.[61] Could it be that if we haven't been obedient in the doing of Jesus's words, we find ourselves crumbling in the move of the Spirit; that when His rain comes and the floods rise and the winds blow, we fall to pieces? The more we build on the Rock, the better we are able to stand in His flow. As James 1:22 states, we need to be "doers of the word, and not hearers only."

Finally, to get the most out of the wind of the Spirit that fills the sails of our life, we need good control of our rudder.

James 3:2-5
2 For we all stumble in many things. If anyone does not stumble in word, he is a perfect man, able also to bridle the whole body.
3 Indeed, we put bits in horses' mouths that they may obey us, and we turn their whole body.
*4 Look also at ships: although they are so large and are driven by fierce winds, they are turned by a very small **rudder** wherever the pilot desires.*
5 Even so the tongue is a little member and boasts great things. See how great a forest a little fire kindles! NKJV

Proper rudder control requires walking by the Spirit, for "no man can tame the tongue."[62] If we have repented, received, proceeded to build on the Rock, and then speak contrary to the Spirit of truth, our ship is sure to shift its course in the wrong direction. But if we confess the truth He breathes within our hearts, we will be true sons of the Spirit blowing where He sends us.

---

[61] The Spirit brings life. "Slain in the Spirit" is worse than an oxymoron. Charismatic Anglicans and Catholics use the more polite term "resting in the Spirit."
[62] James 3:8 NKJV.

CHAPTER 3

Water

The fountain of living waters

Water permeates Scripture. In a single brainstorming session, I jotted down the following water-related words in the Bible: Water, sea, stream, river, mist, snow, hail, ice, deep, well, spring, fountain, laver, baptism, flow, pour, drink, wave, overflow, and flood. This list isn't exhaustive, but a concordance search would lead to over 1,400 uses in the King James Version—not to mention the subsequent searches based on the original language words. The Bible is far from a dry read.

Water confronts us from the very beginning: "In the beginning God created the Heaven and the earth. And the earth was without form, and void; and darkness was upon the face of the deep. And the Spirt of God moved upon the face of the waters." Thus commences Genesis and the creation account.[63]

Genesis 1:3
And God said, Let there be light: and there was light.

The very first thing that the Light of God illuminated was the face of the waters. I believe this is telling. Jesus is the light of world.[64] The last lessons He taught His disciples, both before the crucifixion and

---

[63] Pop quiz: what day was water created?
[64] John 1:9; 3:19; 8:12; 9:5; 12:46.

just prior to His ascension, were centered on the Holy Spirit.[65] Though the subject of the Holy Spirit is mysterious and murky to many Evangelicals and confounding to unbelievers in general, it certainly isn't His intention to stay obscure. The Godhead wants us to know Him, and He wants to flow through us. It is His washing that cleanses us and His watering that causes fruit to grow in our lives. Look at me—hose on full blast without properly preparing the ground first. Let me establish the symbol before we go any deeper.

A Well in Samaria

John 4:7-10

7 There cometh a woman of Samaria to draw water: Jesus saith unto her, Give me to drink.

8 (For his disciples were gone away unto the city to buy meat.)

9 Then saith the woman of Samaria unto him, How is it that thou, being a Jew, askest drink of me, which am a woman of Samaria? for the Jews have no dealings with the Samaritans.

10 Jesus answered and said unto her, If thou knewest the gift of God, and who it is that saith to thee, Give me to drink; thou wouldest have asked of him, and he would have given thee living water.

The gift of God, Romans informs us, is eternal life through Jesus Christ our Lord.[66] In this encounter at the well of Jacob, Jesus employs the living water metaphor for the born-again experience.

John 4:11-14

11 The woman saith unto him, Sir, thou hast nothing to draw with, and the well is deep: from whence then hast thou that living water?

12 Art thou greater than our father Jacob, which gave us the well, and drank thereof himself, and his children, and his cattle?

13 Jesus answered and said unto her, Whosoever drinketh of this water shall thirst again:

---

[65] John 14-16; Luke 24:49; John 20:19-23; Acts 1:1-9.
[66] Rom. 6:23.

61

14 But whosoever drinketh of the water that I shall give him shall never thirst; but the water that I shall give him shall be in him a well [Greek *pege*, a fountain or well] *of water springing up into everlasting life.*

After offering the living water, Jesus describes how to receive it in an extension of the metaphor. One must drink the water (receive it), and it then becomes a well of water (continuously supplied) springing up into everlasting life (it has outflow and impact).

The Feast of Tabernacles and the Washing of the Holy Spirit
Jesus next employed the living water metaphor during the feast of tabernacles. It was on the last day, the great day of the feast, that Jesus decided to make his announcement. The priests circled the altar seven times, proclaiming, "Save now, O Lord! O Lord, give prosperity!"[67] For the last time of the festival, a priest tipped the golden pitcher, pouring out water gathered from the pool of Siloam. The temple choir finished the Hallel[68] on floating flute notes[69] flowing from the musicians. The people waved their willow bows and palm branches in worship as the priests gave three blasts from their silver trumpets. In the expectant hush that followed, Jesus shouted.

John 7:37b-39
37 ... If any man thirst, let him come unto me, and drink.
38 He that believeth on me, as the scripture hath said, out of his belly shall flow rivers of living water.
39 (But this spake he of the Spirit, which they that believe on him should receive: for the Holy Ghost was not yet given; because that Jesus was not yet glorified.)

---

[67] Ps. 118:25.
[68] Ps. 113 – 118.
[69] Flutes are pierced instruments, their sound a call to consider Christ on the cross.

The "rivers of living water" was the Holy Ghost that was going to be poured out. The entire ceremony was understood to be representative of the outpouring of the Holy Spirit.

> "[The ceremony of the pouring out of water on the altar during the Feast of Tabernacles had] . . . its main and real application . . . to the future outpouring of the Holy Spirit, as predicted—probably in allusion to this very rite—by Isaiah the prophet. Thus the Talmud says distinctly: 'Why is the name of it called, the drawing out of water? Because of the pouring out of the Holy Spirit, according to what is said: 'With joy shall ye draw water out of the wells of salvation.'"[70]

This understanding of the Holy Spirit's role in salvation was expressed by the apostle Paul in his pastoral letter to Titus.

Titus 3:4-6
4 But after that the kindness and love of God our Saviour toward man appeared,
5 Not by works of righteousness which we have done, but according to his mercy he saved us, by the washing of regeneration, and renewing of the Holy Ghost;
6 Which he shed on us abundantly through Jesus Christ our Saviour;

He saved us through the washing of regeneration and renewing of the Holy Spirit. The Greek word translated "washing" is *lautron*, which is a basin or laver for washing. One could call it a baptismal. The "washing of regeneration" stands parallel to "renewing of the Holy Ghost." The former is the symbolic language of the latter. This correlation echoes the testimony of John the Baptist.

---

[70] Alfred Edersheim, *The Temple: Its Ministries and Services*, Updated Edition, Hendrickson Publishers, Peabody, Mass., 1994, p. 220-222. The Isaiah reference is Isaiah 12:1-3.

Mark 1:8
I indeed have baptized you with water: but he shall baptize you with the Holy Ghost.

Isaiah prophesied of the Spirit's role in cleansing and watering as well.

Isaiah 4:4
When the Lord shall have washed away the filth of the daughters of Zion, and shall have purged the blood of Jerusalem from the midst thereof by the spirit of judgment, and by the spirit of burning.

Isaiah 44:3
For I will pour water upon him that is thirsty, and floods upon the dry ground: I will pour my spirit upon thy seed, and my blessing upon thine offspring:

Joel, the prophet that Peter quoted on the day of Pentecost,[71] used this motif also.

Joel 2:23, 28-29
23 Be glad then, ye children of Zion, and rejoice in the Lord your God: for he hath given you the former rain moderately, and he will cause to come down for you the rain, the former rain, and the latter rain in the first month.
28 And it shall come to pass afterward, that I will pour out my spirit upon all flesh; and your sons and your daughters shall prophesy, your old men shall dream dreams, your young men shall see visions:
29 And also upon the servants and upon the handmaids in those days will I pour out my spirit.

Rivers, wells, springs, baptism, and rain all tell us of the watery wonders of the Holy Spirit. The Spirit is letting us know that He is life it-

---

[71] Acts 2:16-18.

self. In extreme cases, a person can survive for up to seventy-three days without food. However, without water, a person will only make it as long as five days or die in the space of a few short hours. The Spirit is the life giver. Without Him, one is spiritually dead—as dead as any plant without water.

Water In and Out
Water cleanses and replenishes. We bathe in it and drink it. We need it to maintain our hygiene as well as our health. It is the same with the Holy Spirit.

1 Corinthians 12:13
For by one Spirit are we all baptized into one body, whether we be Jews or Gentiles, whether we be bond or free; and have been all made to drink into one Spirit.

Baptism is for cleansing. And though the baptism of the Holy Spirit is an internal work, it also speaks to us of the Spirit resting *upon* us. When Jesus rose from Jordan's waters, the Spirit descended *upon* Him.[72] The verse above also tells us that we drank the Spirit *in*. The dynamic of the Spirit abiding *upon* us and dwelling *within* us is an aspect highlighted in several of the symbols we will examine.

In view of water, this dwelling *within* can be compared to drinking a tall glass of cool water on a hot summer's day. We can also imagine ourselves as the water fountain in the park offering refreshment to all who come to drink.[73] His indwelling presence brings life to the body of Christ and helps to organize it down to the cellular level, the same as water imbibed maintains us physically. And His reservoir of life becomes a bubbling fountain, bringing blessing, joy, and life to those who drink from it.

---

[72] Matt. 3:16.
[73] Rev. 22:17.

What Is Water?

What is water in the natural? Composed of two hydrogen atoms and one oxygen atom, its molecular structure has to be the most well-known chemical formula in history: H_2O. Due to the covalent bonds between the hydrogen atoms and the oxygen atom and oxygen's high electronegativity, the molecule is bent in a way that leaves the negativity of the oxygen exposed on one end while the hydrogen atoms congregate on the other, creating a positive charge. The fact that water molecules are polarized has much to do with how water behaves. And the electrical qualities of water become exponential in the clouds, but we will have to wait until Chapter 9 to study those.

Water is colorless, tasteless, and odorless. Often times, we can feel the Spirit but not see, taste, or smell Him. Though electrically charged, water is highly stable. The Holy Spirit isn't volatile or erratic. His character and behavior are nothing if not consistent. Water is the only substance on earth that appears naturally in all physical states of matter: solid, liquid, and gas. Correspondingly, the Holy Spirit came to convict the world of sin, righteousness, and judgment.[74]

Water can absorb a tremendous amount of heat and has a very high boiling point, which may be why a watched pot seems to take ages to boil. Patience and temperance are fruits of the Holy Spirit.[75] He does not boil over in anger easily. Water is the best liquid heat conductor except for mercury. The Holy Spirit carries the love of God throughout the body of Christ without toxicity.

Water is the universal solvent. More things dissolve in water than any other substance. The Holy Spirit washes through us, carrying away all impurities. He is the *Holy* Spirit who makes us holy. Through His inner witness of the conviction of sin, righteousness, and judgment, we

---

[74] John 16:7-8.
[75] Gal. 5:22-23.

are cleansed of dead works and formed into servants of righteous-ness.[76]

The Voice of Many Waters and a Dripping Faucet

"Living water" is an idiom for fresh, flowing water. Water has a distinctive sound when it flows. From the drip of a faucet to the roar of a river in the rapids, we know running water when we hear it. Perhaps familiar to most is the description of the Lord's voice sounding like rushing waters.

Ezekiel 43:2
and I saw the glory of the God of Israel coming from the east. His voice was like the roar of rushing waters, and the land was radiant with his glory. NIV

This is how John described the voice he heard when he was in the Spirit on the Lord's day and turned to see the one speaking to him whose voice was "as the sound of many waters" (Rev 1:15). When God speaks to us at this volume, it is momentous and draws attention to His awesome glory. But He has another way of speaking that is insistent, hard to ignore, and even irritating if not acted upon.

Proverbs 27:15-16
15 A continual dripping on a very rainy day And a contentious woman
*   are alike;*
16 Whoever restrains her restrains the wind, And grasps oil with his
*   right hand. NKJV*

I can see you scratching your head, so bear with me a little bit in my folly. Interpreting the Scriptures is a different function than applying them. Of the two, interpretation is the more stringent and narrow discipline. This helps to keep us on solid orthodox ground. But the appli-

---

[76] Ps. 143:10; Rom. 6.

cations of Scripture impact all aspects of life.[77] It is in the use of both that we know not to muzzle the ox that treads the corn (interpretation) and make sure to financially support those working in fulltime ministry (application).[78] In this understanding, let us consider the proverb quoted above.

Solomon compares a quarrelsome wife to the constant dripping on a rainy day. Dripping rain may not irritate you, but I've never met anybody immune to the insistent drip of a faucet. Something about the constant beat of single drops of water landing in miniature splashes disproportionately draws our attention away from louder things. Though rain isn't exclusively a symbol for the Holy Spirit, we should always wonder if He is telling us something about Himself when He mentions it in Scripture. Note Solomon's follow on admonition after the rain: "Whoever restrains her, restrains the *wind*, and grasps *oil* with his right hand."

Both wind and oil are primary symbols for the Holy Spirit. I know Solomon is talking about a quarrelsome wife. But in doing so, he uses three of the most common symbols for the Holy Spirit: rain (water), wind, and oil. Might not the Holy Spirit be trying to teach us something about Himself here? Oftentimes, the quarrelsomeness of the wife is a matter of perspective. Perhaps her husband's conduct is less than exemplary. Desperate for normalcy or even common decency, the wife might fall into the habit of nagging. When such couples come in for counseling, well-intentioned ministers frequently tell the wife, "Listen, you are not the Holy Spirit. It is His job to convict of sin, righteousness, and judgment." What are we saying? We are saying that a wife's nagging is counterproductive, but on the other hand, the Spirit's nagging is unavoidable.

---

[77] 2 Pet. 1:3-4.
[78] 1 Cor. 9:6-14.

Judges 13:24-25

24 And the woman bare a son, and called his name Samson: and the child grew, and the Lord blessed him.

25 And the Spirit of the Lord began to move him at times in the camp of Dan between Zorah and Eshtaol.

The Hebrew word translated "move" in verse 25 is *pa'am* and it means to tap or beat regularly with the idea of agitating or impelling. Think of the Spirit dripping into Samson's heart the need to take action against the Philistines. Like a faucet that needs fixing, this word sent Samson fighting. The idea of words from the Lord falling like drops can be seen in other Scriptures as well.

Amos 7:16

Now therefore hear thou the word of the Lord: Thou sayest, Prophesy not against Israel, and drop not thy word against the house of Isaac.

Through Hebraic parallelism, we see prophesy compared to "dropping a word." The Hebrew terms translated "drop" in the verse above is *nataph* ,and it means to distill gradually, to fall in drops. In Micah 2:6 and 11, it is translated as "prophesy" in the KJV, but I find its use in Job most poetic. Think of your relationship with the Holy Spirit as you read the verses below.

Job 29:21-23

21 Unto me men gave ear, and waited, and kept silence at my counsel.

22 After my words they spake not again; and my speech dropped [nataph] upon them.

23 And they waited for me as for the rain; and they opened their mouth wide as for the latter rain.

The Spirit's voice inside us is often more like dripping water than rushing river. It is in the still small voice that intimacy is built, our insecurities challenged, and orders given.[79] When we listen and obey, we've caught the wind and held the anointing.[80]

Let It Rain

The Holy Spirit's interaction with us as falling rain is different than His baptismal presence or His imbibed essence. We can get glimpses of this in the natural where rain waters the ground and washes the trees. First, we must understand the qualitative difference between getting wet in the rain and deciding to go for a swim. In the baptism, we must decide to enter the water. In drinking, we must take action to bring the water into us. Rain comes of its own accord. We can decide to venture out in it or stay sheltered and dry. Regardless, the rain falls in accordance to God's goodness.[81]

Scripture compares man to both trees and earth. [82] How rain flows through each is instructive of the sovereign moves of the Spirit when He falls like rain. The leaves of deciduous trees commonly intercept 20-30% of the rain that falls on them. Through the process of "stemflow," the architecture of these trees leads the water down the stems, twigs, branches, and trunk to bring additional water into the ground at the base of the tree for the roots. In Figure 3.1, we can see the outpouring of the Holy Spirit as rain washing us and watering our roots to bring depth and growth. But the rain also falls through the canopy as "throughfall," watering the ground around the tree while diffusing the force of its fall. This is a picture of us when, as good stewards, we wisely minister the Holy Spirit's graces to those around us. Such wisdom and restrain in ministry can be seen in Paul's admonition to "lay hands suddenly on no man" (1 Tim. 5:22) and his instructions for well-ordered, Spirit-led meetings (1 Cor. 14). Finally, "canopy drip" waters the ground around the edge of the plant canopy. In

---

[79] 1 Kings 19:11-18.
[80] For more on the anointing, see Chapter 5.
[81] Matt. 5:44-48.
[82] Ps. 1:3; Matt. 13:3-9, 18-23.

this, we see the Spirit's outpouring on His people turning into outreach to the world around them.[83]

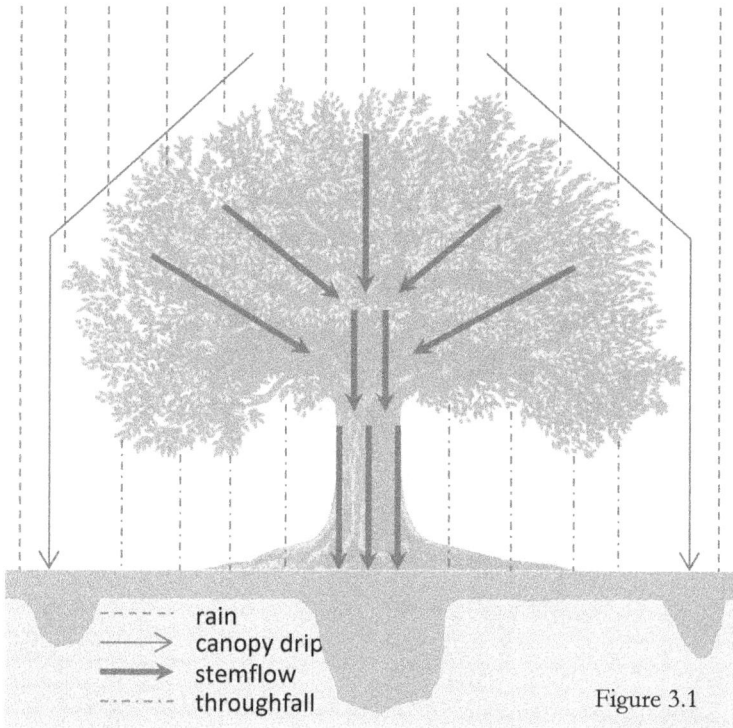

rain
canopy drip
stemflow
throughfall

Figure 3.1

When rain reaches the ground, it begins to infiltrate the soil. The rate of infiltration normally declines rapidly during the early part of a rainstorm event and reaches a constant value after several hours of rainfall.[84] Have you ever been drenched in an outpouring move of the Holy Spirit? Its intensity is overwhelming at times, and it feels like you are rushing down a river to God only knows where. Manifestations are dramatic—miracles, healings, prophecies, spiritual songs—and emotions run high. There is laughter and crying and dancing and falling out. But after a while, things seem to taper off. In comparison to the early days of the outpouring, it almost feels dry. What has happened?

---

[83] Descriptions of rain flow through trees taken from http://www.geog.ouc.bc.ca/physgeog/contents/8k.html, accessed 2/12/2001.
[84] http://www.geog.ouc.bc.ca/physgeog/contents/8l.html, accessed 2/12/2001.

Have we grown cold? Did the rain cease? Has God left us? No. we have simply arrived to a constant rate of infiltration.

The impact of rain can be quite dramatic. Once the constant rate of infiltration has been reached, the overflow runs on the ground. This runoff is visible, exhilarating, and at flood stage, terrifying. Infiltration rates are primarily determined by soil types; for example, shallow soils over rock or soils with high clay content exhibit greater runoff. Correspondingly, a heavy outpouring of the spirit, like at a revival, can exhibit a fair amount of runoff. We watch as people are overcome by the Spirit[85] and fall to the ground, some sob uncontrollably, others manifest demons. What we see as a great move of the Spirit excites us, but we can miss the deeper lasting works of infiltration, percolation, and throughflow. These types of ground flows are illustrated in Figure 3.2 below.

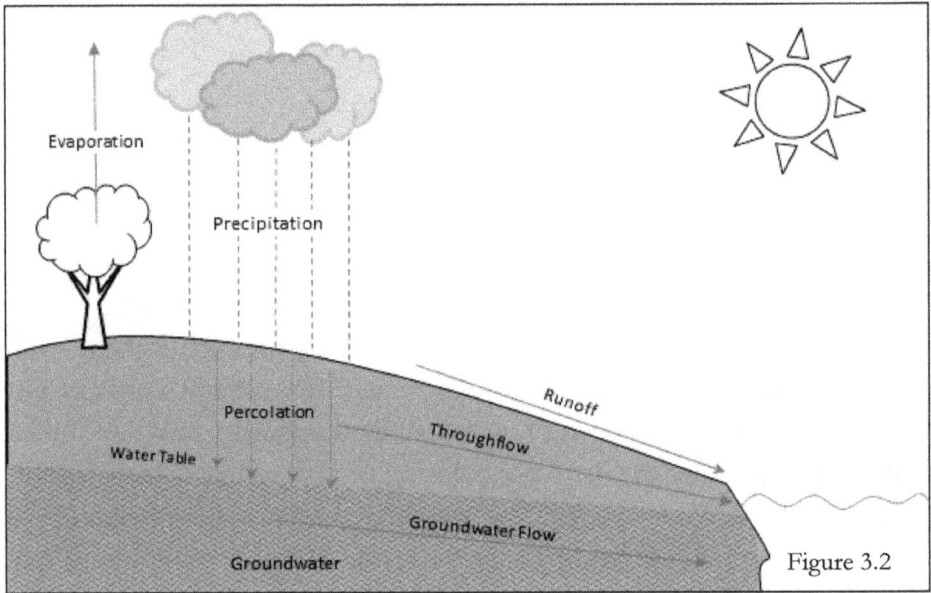

Figure 3.2

---

[85] Commonly called "slain in the Spirit", but I'm not a real fan of the term as most folks get back up. For an example of what happens when someone is indeed slain in the Spirit, read Acts 5.

Infiltration is the overall process of water's move into the ground. Percolation is water's vertical descent to its table. It is through percolation that our deep waters are supplied—our wells filled and our water table raised. Water's motion is always downward, seeking the lowest parts. It precipitates from the heavens and finds its way to the ocean depths, perfectly illustrating the flow of God's grace from heaven's throne to humble hearts hungering and thirsting for righteousness.

Filling requires percolation. Runoff is dramatic, but it is aptly named. It runs off—here today, down the hillside tomorrow. The water that percolates through us fills the belly, from which flow rivers of living water, and collects in the reservoirs that spring up into everlasting life. We need to appreciate this quieter work of the Holy Ghost when He comes in the rainstorm.

The water not only percolates downward, but it also runs horizontally under the soil. This "throughflow" occurs along the downward grade of saturated soil until it reaches a river, lake, or ocean. The waters we cannot contain are meant to move and soak the lowlands around us and collect in the reservoirs that bring abundant life, beauty, and re-creation to others.

We can see the principle of the Cross in water's flow through trees and soil. Christ paid the price for our broken relationship with the Father and His blood brought us access to the Spirit. This is the vertical post of the cross pointing to the first and great commandment to love God with all of our heart, soul, mind, and strength, and it is seen in rain's fall from heaven down the tree trunk to the roots, percolating down the layers of soil to reach the groundwater. Christ also paid the price for our sins against each other and paved the way for the Spirit's love to pour through us. This is the horizontal beam of the cross pointing to the second law of loving our neighbors as ourselves, and this can be seen in a tree's canopy drip and the throughflow of water under the soil.

Treasures in Snow and Ice

Crystallized water brings us to another level of understanding the Holy Spirit. Like Jesus, He has much to tell us. But the amount He wants to share is greater than the amount we can bear at any given moment.[86] He works around this communication problem through frozen words. If He rained it out on us all at once, the runoff would be catastrophic. So instead, He piles up the overflow in fluffy white reservoirs that He melts over time to water the land with streams of grace.

Psalm 147:15-19
15 He sends out His command to the earth; His word runs very swiftly.
16 He gives snow like wool; He scatters the frost like ashes;
17 He casts out His hail like morsels; Who can stand before His cold?
18 He sends out His word and melts them; He causes His wind to blow, and the waters flow.
19 He declares His word to Jacob, His statutes and His judgments to Israel. NKJV

This section of Scripture is rich with instructive parallelisms. Verse 15 frames what follows. I have laid out the parallel structure below.

> v. 15a – He sends out His command to the earth
> - He gives snow like wool – v. 16
> - He scatters the frost like ashes – v. 16
> - He casts out His hail like morsels – v. 17
>
> v. 15b – His word runs very swiftly
> - He sends out His word – v. 18
>   - He causes His wind to blow – v. 18
> - and melts them – v. 18
>   - and the waters flow – v. 18

Under "His command" we have snow, frost, and hail—all frozen types of water with their own similes attached: wool, ashes, and morsels.

---

[86] John 16:12-13.

These commands are melted by His wind (Spirit), which causes the water of these words to flow. Frozen water has limited uses for the ground. After all, Paul didn't write: "I planted, Apollos snowed; but God gave the increase."[87] Watering the ground is certainly the more common idiom. Even so, the uses of snow are highly informative.

Isaiah 1:18
Come now, and let us reason together, saith the Lord: though your sins be as scarlet, they shall be as white as snow; though they be red like crimson, they shall be as wool.

Snow and wool are used in Isaiah 1:18 as symbols of our purity (through their color association) after our sins have been washed away.

Psalm 51:7
Purge me with hyssop, and I shall be clean: wash me, and I shall be whiter than snow.

In comparison to hail, snow falls gently. When the Spirit moves over snow commands, the snowmelt cleanses and refreshes us. It washes away our iniquities through the conviction of sin. In contrast to snow and hail, frost doesn't fall but freezes in place. Snow and hail are frozen water dispensed from heaven. Frost is water frozen on the ground. It is moisture that wasn't absorbed before the cold came. Frost speaks of rejection as well as separateness. It is the element the homeless face and forms the boundary between the heavens.[88]

Genesis 31:40
Thus I was; in the day the drought consumed me, and the frost by night; and my sleep departed from mine eyes.

---

[87] 1 Cor. 3:6.
[88] Ezek. 1:22.

Jeremiah 36:30

[Jehoiakim's] ... dead body shall be cast out in the day to the heat, and in the night to the frost.

When the Holy Spirit waters our hearts with the conviction of righteousness and we grieve Him with a cold-shoulder turn, the words turn frosty. The Psalmist sang of the Lord scattering His frost like ashes.[89] Ashes are a sign of mourning and when combined with sackcloth are emblematic of repentance.[90]

Jeremiah 6:26

*O daughter of my people, gird thee with sackcloth, **and wallow thyself in ashes: make thee mourning** [emphasis added], as for an only son, most bitter lamentation: for the spoiler shall suddenly come upon us.*

God mourns over our sin and yearns for us to repent. When we respond to His calling, words we have frozen with our rejection melt and water our souls, infusing them with righteousness.

Hail falls as a judgment of God. This is most clearly seen in the Exodus story of the plague of hail (Exodus 9:13-34). Pharaoh refused to let God's people go to worship Him. God rains down His Spirit in response to worship.[91] Hail is formed when falling rain encounters powerful updrafts, causing it to travel into the freezing parts of the cloud. This process repeats itself, building the hail layer upon layer, until its size overcomes the updraft and succumbs to gravity. Then it falls, not as a life-giving rain but as a painful stoning from heaven. When we continuously reject the grace that the Spirit rains down upon us, He ultimately moves down in judgment.

The Psalmist says that the Lord casts hail out as "morsels." The Hebrew word is *path* and is frequently used for pieces of bread or por-

---

[89] Ps. 147:16.
[90] See Job 42:6; Dan. 9:3-7; and Matt. 11:21.
[91] Joel 2:23; John 7:39.

tions of the grain offering. Even in judgment, God's words are bread to live by. Jesus's response to the devil when tempted to make bread[92] was the lesson the Lord was teaching Israel in the wilderness when He fed them with manna for forty years. Exodus 16:14 informs us that manna was like frost on the ground. It even appeared in the same fashion as frost, in tandem with the dew.[93] Though this mixes the metaphor, it shows that God considers His "ice words" no less bread for their frozenness. If they are gathered, prepared, and ingested like manna (as daily bread), they bring life.

The Dust of the Ground Is Wet Clay
Though our frame is dust,[94] up to 60% of the adult human body is water. Our brains and hearts are 73% water. Our lungs are over 80% water. Even our hardest parts, our bones, are 31% H_2O. We can dry our hands all we want, but our skin will still be 64% water.[95] The various ways water keeps our bodies alive illustrate how the Holy Spirit brings life to the body of Christ. Consider the following:

- Water helps deliver oxygen all over the body. The Holy Spirit breathes life into us.
- Water allows the body's cells to grow, reproduce, and survive.[96] The Holy Spirit deepens our walk with Christ, leads us in evangelism, and guides us through life.
- Water converts food to the components needed for survival. Its presence in our blood metabolizes carbohydrates and proteins and transports them to the cells where the nutrients can be used. The Holy Spirit brings understanding to the same words He inspired holy men to write when He was revealing the

---

[92] See Matt. 4:4, which is the lesson of manna which covered the ground like frost.
[93] Num. 11:9.
[94] Gen. 2:7; Ps. 103:14.
[95] https://water.usgs.gov/edu/propertyyou.html, accessed 3/28/17.
[96] Examples from physiology taken from https://water.usgs.gov/edu/propertyyou.html, accessed 3/28/17.

Scriptures to them. These words can then be properly digested in the body of Christ for spiritual nourishment and growth.

- Water acts as a shock absorber to the brain and spinal column. The Holy Spirit's direction cushions the administrative gifts in the body of Christ so they can function without damage.
- Water regulates our body temperature. One of the fruits of the Spirit is temperance.
- Water lubricates our joints. The unity of the Spirit helps keep the body fitly joined together.[97]
- Water flushes waste out of our bodies. The Spirit actively works in us to be holy even as He is Holy.[98]

Supply and Demand

We are not the only living creatures composed mostly of water. Without water, there would be no life on earth. The biosphere lives and breathes because of water. When we think of all living things being primarily water, it is instructive to see the percentage of the total supply they take up. The entire biosphere—all plants and animals—only contains 0.00004% of Earth's water supply even though most of its members are individually composed of over 50% water. In contrast, the oceans contain 97.25% of Earth's water. Compared to the supply available, an individual's amount of water is statistically insignificant. We know the Holy Spirit is limitless, but it helps to see quantifiable comparisons because infinity cannot be imagined. He has all the water you need and then some.[99]

---

[97] Eph. 4:3-7, 16.
[98] Eph. 1:3-14; Titus 3:5; 1 Pet. 1:16.
[99] Water reservoir percentages taken from
http://www.physicalgeography.net/fundamentals/8b.html, accessed 4/4/17.

CHAPTER 4

Fire

Freedom in the heavenly flames

How would you describe color to a man born blind? If you had to explain red, green, or blue to a blind man, how would you do it? One approach would be to access the other senses as analogs for sight. Red tastes like cinnamon, smells like roses, feels hot, and sounds like fire. Green tastes like spearmint, smells like fresh cut grass, feels like lettuce leaves, and sounds like wind through the trees. Blue tastes like berries, smells like hyacinth, feels like cool water, and sounds like a saxophone. All these examples would help a blind mind have a better idea of how these colors make us feel. But would the blind man understand color?

In this same way, symbolic language in Scripture helps us have a better idea of the attributes and qualities of our invisible God. Though the Holy Spirit is invisible, He wants us to look toward Him.[100] We are blind with no experience of color and no ability to see it. The Holy Spirit comes alongside us and says, "I blow like the breeze, flow like a fountain, glow like fire." We still can't see Him, but we begin to get a sense of how He approaches us and how we should approach Him.

Deuteronomy 4:24
For the Lord thy God is a consuming fire, even a jealous God.[101]

---

[100] 2 Cor. 4:18; Heb. 11:27.
[101] See also Heb. 12:29.

Right away we should understand that the Holy Spirit is not to be trifled with. In the natural, fire is a useful friend that can give us heat, transform metals, cook food, and even be converted to electricity. But only a fool would treat fire carelessly. In the contest of flesh versus fire, fire wins. Let us keep that in mind as we proceed.

The Likeness of a Fiery Man
When Scripture informs us that our God is a consuming fire, then we should expect to see the Father, Son, and Holy Spirit show up in fiery form. This is exactly what we find.

Ezekiel 1:26-28
26 And above the firmament that was over their heads was the likeness of a throne, as the appearance of a sapphire stone: and upon the likeness of the throne was the likeness as the appearance of a man above upon it.
27 And I saw as the colour of amber, as the appearance of fire round about within it, from the appearance of his loins even upward, and from the appearance of his loins even downward, I saw as it were the appearance of fire, and it had brightness round about.
28 As the appearance of the bow that is in the cloud in the day of rain, so was the appearance of the brightness round about. This was the appearance of the likeness of the glory of the Lord. And when I saw it, I fell upon my face, and I heard a voice of one that spake.

In this vision of the Father, Ezekiel sees Him as a fiery man seated on the throne. From His loins down and from His loins up, He glowed with the brightness of fire. What about the Son?

Revelation 1:13-16
13 and in the midst of the seven lampstands One like the Son of Man, clothed with a garment down to the feet and girded about the chest with a golden band.
14 His head and hair were white like wool, as white as snow, and His eyes like a flame of fire;

15 His feet were like fine brass, as if refined in a furnace, and His voice as the sound of many waters;

16 He had in His right hand seven stars, out of His mouth went a sharp two-edged sword, and His countenance was like the sun shining in its strength. NKJV

John got a preview of the glorified Christ on the Mount of Transfiguration.[102] In the vision above, he sees Him as never before: eyes aflame, feet fresh from the furnace, and His face bright as the sun. "When I saw him," John says, "I fell down at his feet like a dead man."[103] This description of Jesus bears a striking resemblance to the description of the Father we read in Ezekiel. We know that man was made in the image of God, and most of us are not surprised to find the Father or Son show up in the "appearance of a man," but what about the Spirit?

Ezekiel 8:2-3

*2 Then I looked, and behold, **a form that had the appearance of a man**. Below what appeared to be his waist was **fire**, and above his waist was something like the appearance of brightness, like gleaming metal.*

*3 He put out the form of a hand and took me by a lock of my head, and **the Spirit lifted me up** between earth and heaven and brought me in visions of God to Jerusalem, to the entrance of the gateway of the inner court that faces north, where was the seat of the image of jealousy, which provokes to jealousy. ESV* [Emphasis added.]

After describing the form of a fiery man putting his hand out and grabbing Ezekiel by his hair, the prophet tells us who it was that picked him up. "The Spirit lifted me up," he says. Here in Ezekiel we have a clear picture of the Holy Spirit that mirrors the descriptions of

---

[102] See Matt. 17:1-2.
[103] Rev. 1:17.

the Father and the Son in His glory. They all have the likeness of a fiery man.

The Spirit of Fire

The Holy Spirit shows up in fire throughout Scripture. Isaiah helps us understand which aspect of His three-fold ministry[104] He is highlighting in the flames.

Isaiah 4:4
The Lord will wash away the filth of the women of Zion; he will cleanse the bloodstains from Jerusalem by a spirit of judgment and a spirit of fire. NIV

It is as fire that the Holy Spirit convicts the world of judgment. Judgment consumes the offense as well as the offender. John the Baptist spoke of this when he prophesied about Messiah's mission.

Matthew 3:11-12
11 I indeed baptize you with water unto repentance, but He who is coming after me is mightier than I, whose sandals I am not worthy to carry. He will baptize you with the Holy Spirit and fire.
12 His winnowing fan is in His hand, and He will thoroughly clean out His threshing floor, and gather His wheat into the barn; but He will burn up the chaff with unquenchable fire." NKJV

As the Holy Spirit's wind blows the lifeless husks from the threshing floor of our lives, His fire burns away the heavier strangling straw of our flesh,[105] leaving us with fruitful seeds to sow and increase our fruits of righteousness. When we allow the cleansing flames of the Spirit to free us in this life, our baptism of fire in the next will result in greater reward.

---

[104] Conviction of sin, righteousness, and judgment – see John 16:8-11.
[105] 1 Pet. 1:24.

Daniel 7:9-10

9 I beheld till the thrones were cast down, and the Ancient of days did sit, whose garment was white as snow, and the hair of his head like the pure wool: his throne was like the fiery flame, and his wheels as burning fire.

10 A fiery stream issued and came forth from before him: thousand thousands ministered unto him, and ten thousand times ten thousand stood before him: the judgment was set, and the books were opened.

While an examination of the full end times' implications of this passage is outside of the scope of this work, to see the stream of the Holy Spirit issuing out of the throne of the Ancient of days as a river of fire on the day of judgment is certainly within it. The Spirit of fire tries our works.

1 Corinthians 3:13-15

13 Every man's work shall be made manifest: for the day shall declare it, because it shall be revealed by fire; and the fire shall try every man's work of what sort it is.

14 If any man's work abide which he hath built thereupon, he shall receive a reward.

15 If any man's work shall be burned, he shall suffer loss: but he himself shall be saved; yet so as by fire.

As Jesus said, every sacrifice will be salted with fire.[106]

Fire and Sacrifice

Throughout the Old Testament, God showed His acceptance of a sacrifice by lighting the altar fire. From the burning lamp and smoking furnace that walked through Abram's offering, to the lit altars before the tabernacle and temple and the dramatic confrontation between Elijah

---

[106] Mark 9:49.

and the prophets of Baal,[107] the fire of God landed on the sacrifice and caused it to rise toward the heavens in smoke. On the day of Pentecost, the apostles were gathered together at the hour of prayer as living sacrifices, and the Holy Spirit came in fire.

Acts 2:1-4
1 And when the day of Pentecost was fully come, they were all with one accord in one place.
2 And suddenly there came a sound from heaven as of a rushing mighty wind, and it filled all the house where they were sitting.
3 And there appeared unto them cloven tongues like as of fire, and it sat upon each of them.
4 And they were all filled with the Holy Ghost, and began to speak with other tongues, as the Spirit gave them utterance.

Have you ever seen this scene represented as singular flames of fire sprouting from the heads of the disciples gathered as if each one was his own butane lighter? This view is understandable if it is framed in the language of the Authorized Version. But the Greek word translated "cloven" paints a different picture. The word is *diamerizomenai*, which is the present middle voice of *diamerizoo*, "to cleave asunder, to cut in pieces." The middle voice of this verb is better translated "parting asunder." Robertson citing Hackett states, "the fire-like appearance presented itself at first, as it were, in a single body, and then suddenly parted in this direction and that direction; so that a portion of it rested upon each of those present."[108]

What appeared on the day of Pentecost was a manifestation of the column of fire that flared out to the apostles and rested upon them, letting them know that the promise of the Father had finally come. Jesus had

---

[107] Gen. 15:9-17; Lev. 9:24; 2 Chr. 7:1; 1 Kings 18:30-39 respectively.
[108] from *Robertson's Word Pictures in the New Testament, Electronic Database.* Copyright © 1997, 2003, 2005, 2006 by Biblesoft, Inc. Robertson's Word Pictures in the New Testament. Copyright © 1985 by Broadman Press.

poured out the Holy Spirit to them, even as he said he would.[109] The column of fire is the nighttime manifestation of the column of cloud, which we will examine in depth in Chapter 9. For now, let us content ourselves with a look at the fire from heaven.

Lessons in the Lightning

The Ten Commandments and *Raiders of the Lost Ark* contain Hollywood images of the fire of God. While some aspects of DeMille's and Spielberg's visons may be correct, they can cloud our minds to the obvious pictures God presents to us in Scripture and nature.

Exodus 19:16
*And it came to pass on the third day in the morning, that there were thunders and **lightnings**, and a thick cloud upon the mount, and the voice of the trumpet exceeding loud; so that all the people that was in the camp trembled.* [Emphasis added.]

The Lord announced His arrival on Mr. Sinai with a thundercloud. The Holy Spirit has much to teach us in the cumulonimbus. For now, we will focus on the fires within it.

Psalm 97:1-4
1 The Lord reigneth; let the earth rejoice; let the multitude of isles be glad thereof.
2 Clouds and darkness are round about him: righteousness and judgment are the habitation of his throne.
3 A fire goeth before him, and burneth up his enemies round about.
4 His lightnings enlightened the world: the earth saw, and trembled.

Considering how long lightning has been around, it is amazing that it was not until Benjamin Franklin's historic kite flight that the modern age had proof of its electrical nature. Lightning is powerful and frightening, and its effects can prove deadly.

---

[109] John 16:7 ; Acts 1:4-8; 2:33.

2 Kings 1:10

*And Elijah answered and said to the captain of fifty, If I be a man of God, then **let fire come down from heaven**, and consume thee and thy fifty. And there came down **fire from heaven**, and consumed him and his fifty.* [Emphasis added.]

"Fire from heaven" is something anyone who has ever watched a thunderstorm has seen. How is it produced? Updrafts in the thundercloud carry water particles with them that collide with larger water particles falling down to earth, causing a loss and gain of electrons between them. Eventually, the cloud develops a net positive charge near its top and a net negative charge at the bottom. The entire cloud begins to take on the same polarity in the macro that a single water molecule exhibits in the micro. The charge separation produces millions of volts of electrical potential. Once this potential overcomes the electrical resistance in the air, a flash begins and steps its way down to earth. In typical cloud-to-ground lightning, a streamer is launched from the earth and intercepts the stepped ladder of the lightning bolt just before it reaches the ground.[110] Earth has grabbed Heaven's reach, resulting in a powerful display of light that can change night into day in the blink of an eye.

Fire from heaven is never silent. After the lightshow, we always hear its voice. The electrical discharge heats the air surrounding the lightning channel up to 20,000°C, three times hotter than the surface of the Sun. This produces a shock wave that decays to an acoustic wave as it propagates away from the lightning channel.[111] Thunder rolls and the earth rocks.

These powerful storms equalize the electricity between the atmosphere and the earth. In the natural object lesson of the thunderstorm, God

---

[110] Lightning facts are taken from
https://lightning.nsstc.nasa.gov/primer/primer2.html, accessed 4/24/2017.
[111] Ibid.

plays before our eyes and ears what happens in the spirit realm when the Spirit of fire moves.

Revelation 8:3-5
3 And another angel came and stood at the altar, having a golden censer; and there was given unto him much incense, that he should offer it with the prayers of all saints upon the golden altar which was before the throne.
4 And the smoke of the incense, which came with the prayers of the saints, ascended up before God out of the angel's hand.
5 And the angel took the censer, and filled it with fire of the altar, and cast it into the earth: and there were voices, and thunderings, and lightnings, and an earthquake.

The prayers of the saints ascending are like the updrafts of wind in the cloud. As our requests rise up, His grace pours down. The cleansing fire from the altar overcomes the resistance from the prince and power of the air and wickedness in high places with revelatory flashes of light inspiring the shouts of victory that shake the earth.

Consuming Fire
Wood fueled the altars of God. Isaac climbed Mount Moriah shouldering the wood for Abraham's fire, the sons of Aaron placed wood on the fire of the brazen altar, and Elijah laid the wood in order on the stacked stones atop Mount Carmel. Wet or dry, wood requires three things to burst into flames: heat, air, and uninhibited free radical[112] combination. Heat energy releases the hydrocarbons in the wood, which combine with the oxygen in the air, producing water vapor, carbon monoxide, and carbon dioxide. These chemical reactions give us heat and light because they release more energy than they use. Once sufficient heat energy has been applied to the wood, combustion is a

---

[112] Free radicals are atoms or a group of atoms containing at least one unpaired electron and having a short lifetime before reacting to form a stable molecule.

self-sustaining chain reaction. So long as air and fuel remain present, the fire keeps burning.

The natural requirements of combustion illustrate for us our fiery relationship with the Holy Spirit. We are the wood and the sacrifice. Romans 12:1 admonishes us to present our bodies as living sacrifices unto God. There is no need to light a barren altar—no sacrifice, no fire. Both the wood and the sacrifice are cold and dead. Heat is necessary to quicken them, to energetically release what has been offered into radical combination with the Breath that lights them. As we have seen, it is God Himself who brings the heat and lights the fire. But once the fire is lit, we bear the responsibility of keeping it burning.

Leviticus 6:12-13
12 And the fire upon the altar shall be burning in it; it shall not be put
out: and the priest shall burn wood on it every morning, and lay
the burnt offering in order upon it; and he shall burn thereon the
fat of the peace offerings.
13 The fire shall ever be burning upon the altar; it shall never go out.

Once offered on the altar, we should stay there. Being a living sacrifice means living sacrificially. It means joining Jesus in the submissive sonship prayer: "not as I will, but as You will." It means esteeming the other as better than ourselves. It means being a doer of the Word and not a hearer only. It means loving in deed and in truth.

When fuel and flame meet, they need oxygen for the fire to burn. The Holy Wind Himself is the air supply in the spiritual furnace of the new birth and the body of Christ. Even as oxygen combines with the hydrocarbons in wood to produce water, smoke, and fire gases, so the Holy Spirit's presence in us brings forth living water, intercessory worship, and the sweet-smelling savor of sacrifice to our God.[113]

---

[113] Living water: John 7:37-39, Intercessory worship: John 4:24; Isa. 6:3-4; 2 Chr. 5:13-14; Rev. 8:3-4, Sweet smell: Eph. 5:1-2; 2 Cor. 2:14-15.

In the natural, adequate combustion requires the three Ts: time, temperature, and turbulence. The same is true in our spiritual lives. Those seriously desirous of spiritual matters generally understand the need to invest the time. Most are appreciative of the increased temperature of their love and fellowship this brings. But turbulence is not something that any of us naturally embraces. Great fires roar because they have fantastic airflow—dynamic turbulence in confined spaces. Without turbulence, the fire dies, because turbulence is what moves the free radicals.

Fire needs uninhibited free-radical combinations to continue burning. Free radicals, an atom or a group of atoms containing at least one unpaired electron, are bits of energized matter bouncing around looking to join other atoms or molecules to form stable compounds. Uninhibited free radical combination is a dynamic picture of evangelism and new church formation. The Spirit is the ignition fire to the flames of the church. Where the Spirit of the Lord is, there is liberty—a radical freedom to go and grow where God sends. As His wind fans us into flames, we are energetically released to seek out others in need and combine with them, bringing God's stabilizing grace into their lives. These combinations release more energy than they use.

Light and Heat

Fire radiates light and heat. As the lampstand in the holy place lit the table of showbread, even so the Holy Spirit illuminates the Scripture that reveals the bread from heaven, the Lord Jesus Christ.[114] As a fire cheers a home and warms the body, so the Holy Spirit spreads the warmth and strength of His love. Romans 12:11 tells us to be "aglow and burning with the Spirit."[115] As light dispels darkness, heat dispels cold. It always flows from the hotter (higher) energy state to the colder

---

[114] 1 Cor. 2:9-13; Eph. 1:17-23.

[115] The definite article is present in the Greek, pointing to *the* Holy Spirit. The wording is from the Amplified Version.

(lower) energy state. This happens through radiation, conduction, and convection.

Radiation is heat transference through electromagnetic waves that carry the energy away from the emitting object. Our planet receives most of its heat from solar radiation. When we feel the warmth of the Sun on our face, we are being bathed in its radiated thermal energy. Examples of spiritual radiation abound in Scripture. Jesus on the Mount of Transfiguration radiated the glory of God.[116] Stephen's face shone like an angel's when the Sanhedrin put him on trial.[117] Moses came down from Mount Sinai with face aglow; a sight frightening enough to the Israelites that he had to wear a veil.[118] The Spirit imparts His zeal and fervor to us through the radiated glory of Christ.

2 Corinthians 3:17-18
17 Now the Lord is that Spirit: and where the Spirit of the Lord is, there is liberty.
18 But we all, with open face beholding as in a glass the glory of the Lord, are changed into the same image from glory to glory, even as by the Spirit of the Lord.

This changed-image glorification process is God working in us to willingly work for His good pleasure. As we obey and submit to the radiated glory of the Spirit, we are empowered to shine as lights in the world.[119]

Conduction requires physical touch. When material possessing a greater level of kinetic energy comes in contact with one of a lower level, it transfers its energy through direct molecular collision. Higher-speed particles collide with slower speed particles, increasing the kinetic energy of the slower-speed particles. Energy is imparted through

---

[116] Matt. 17:2.
[117] Acts 6:15.
[118] Exod. 34:29-35.
[119] Phil. 2:13-16.

contact that allows the vibration of the hotter element to affect the colder one. We can see spiritual conduction at work in the laying on of hands. Paul reminded Timothy to fan into flame the gift of God that was in him through Paul's laying on of hands.[120]

Convection is heat transference through fluid motion. When fluids such as air or liquids are heated and move away from the heat source, they carry thermal energy with them. The motion occurs because the fluid near the heat source becomes less dense—freer and more active—causing the colder fluid to fall. The falling fluid displaces the hotter fluid, in essence pushing it upward. This is why oil and water boil up and hot air rises.

We experience the convective heat of the Holy Spirit most in the assembly of the saints. Scripture admonishes us to not forsake the assembly of the saints for this very reason. We are to gather together in consideration of each other to "provoke unto love and to good works" (Heb. 10:24-25). The Greek word translated "provoke" is *paroxusmos* and means "to stir up." The heat of expressed Holy Spirit encouragement warms the atmosphere of the assembly, bringing comfort and edification and spurring a deeper worship of God.[121]

As we walk in the Spirit, He leads us through all of these warming adventures: radiating His love, conducting His power, and stirring up the hearts of those around us. Our response to His fiery nature increases our luminescence and the fervency of our compassion.

The Spirit's Convicting Work
Receiving a conviction is bad when it comes with a subsequent sentence, when we are being punished *after* wrongdoing. But convictions *before* the act can save us from self-destruction. This is the work of the

---

[120] 2 Tim. 1:6 ESV. The laying on of hands is one of the foundational principles of the doctrine of Christ, see Heb. 6:1-2.
[121] 1 Cor. 14:1-5, 24-25.

Holy Spirit. As the voice and advocate for Jesus Christ, He helps us to know what is wrong so we can avoid it and choose the right way.

John 16:7-11
7 Nevertheless I tell you the truth. It is to your advantage that I go away; for if I do not go away, the Helper will not come to you; but if I depart, I will send Him to you.
8 And when He has come, He will convict the world of sin, and of righteousness, and of judgment:
9 of sin, because they do not believe in Me;
10 of righteousness, because I go to My Father and you see Me no more;
11 of judgment, because the ruler of this world is judged. NKJV

He convicts—convinces the world through persuasive argument—of its sin, Jesus's righteousness, and God's judgment. Though He is fully active working this way with us our entire lives, the sequence also illustrates the progression of our journey with Him. Before we came to saving faith in Jesus, we were of the world. The Holy Spirit worked with us, exposing our sin and our need for the Savior. When Jesus was on earth teaching the disciples, He would personally instruct them in proper behavior—what to do and what not to do. The Spirit now carries out this sanctifying work in the conviction of righteousness, informing us in His still small voice, "This is the way, walk ye in it."[122] The conviction of judgment is the Holy Spirit leading us in the executive function of the kingdom, ". . . because the ruler of this world is judged." When we follow His lead in judgment, demons are cast out, diseases are healed, and captives are delivered.

In a general sense, the three broadest symbols of the Holy Spirit in Scripture—wind, water, and fire—give reference to His convicting work. Wind speaks of the conviction of sin, water of the conviction of righteousness, and fire of the conviction of judgment. Fire is the pri-

---

[122] Isa. 30:21.

mary symbol and tool of God's judgment. But let us never forget who the ultimate focus of this judgment is: the ruler of this world, the devil.

1 John 3:8
He that committeth sin is of the devil; for the devil sinneth from the beginning. For this purpose the Son of God was manifested, that he might destroy the works of the devil.

Jesus sent the Holy Spirit to continue His devil-destroying work on the earth through us. The Spirit's convicting judgment fire purifies and refines us, burns the bonds that bind us, and tries our works so we may have our full reward.

Purifying and Refining Fire

According to Levitical law, clothing infected with mildew had to be brought to the priest for inspection. After examining it, the priest would set it aside for seven days. He would then inspect it again. If the mildew had grown, the article had to be burned. If not, it could be washed.[123] As we saw in Chapter 3, the Holy Spirit washes through us like water. But there are things in our lives that resist simple washing, things that need to be burned away so we can be purified and free.

Numbers 31:21-23
21 And Eleazar the priest said unto the men of war which went to the battle, This is the ordinance of the law which the Lord commanded Moses;
22 Only the gold, and the silver, the brass, the iron, the tin, and the lead,
23 Every thing that may abide the fire, ye shall make it go through the fire, and it shall be clean: nevertheless it shall be purified with the water of separation: and all that abideth not the fire ye shall make go through the water.

---

[123] Lev. 13:47-59 NIV.

The spoils of war had to be cleansed to be used. Items that could not withstand fire had to go through water. But all metals had to be melted down, their former image and purpose transformed through the refiner's fire. Once pulled from the flames, the metals were tempered in the water of separation, which contained the ashes of the red heifer sacrifice suspended in it. Even the cleansing water contained symbolic fire within it.

Malachi 3:2-3

2 But who may abide the day of his coming? and who shall stand when he appeareth? for he is like a refiner's fire, and like fullers' soap:

3 And he shall sit as a refiner and purifier of silver: and he shall purify the sons of Levi, and purge them as gold and silver, that they may offer unto the Lord an offering in righteousness.

Priests of the kingdom are not exempt from this refining and purifying process. The Holy Spirit's fire is at work in us to cleanse us of every impure motive and thought so that the works we carry to the judgment seat of Christ stand to be rewarded.[124]

Burning the Bonds that Bind Us

Shadrach's, Meshach's, and Abednego's refusal to bow down to Nebuchadnezzar's idol infuriated the king. Enraged, he ordered the furnace heated seven times higher than customary. Fully dressed and bound, the three friends were thrown into flames fearsome enough to fry the life out of their guards.

Daniel 3:24-25

24 Then King Nebuchadnezzar was astonished; and he rose in haste and spoke, saying to his counselors, "Did we not cast three men bound into the midst of the fire?" They answered and said to the king, "True, O king."

---

[124] 1 Cor. 3:12-15.

25 "Look!" he answered, "I see four men loose, walking in the midst of the fire; and they are not hurt, and the form of the fourth is like the Son of God." NKJV

These men went into the fire bound, but all that burned were the bonds that bound them. The Son of God stood with them in the fire as its flames set them free. As dramatic as this narrative is, I am only using it to illustrate the principle that is more directly played out in the book of Judges.

Judges 15:11-13
11 Then three thousand men of Judah went to the top of the rock Etam, and said to Samson, Knowest thou not that the Philistines are rulers over us? what is this that thou hast done unto us? And he said unto them, As they did unto me, so have I done unto them.
12 And they said unto him, We are come down to bind thee, that we may deliver thee into the hand of the Philistines. And Samson said unto them, Swear unto me, that ye will not fall upon me yourselves.
13 And they spake unto him, saying, No; but we will bind thee fast, and deliver thee into their hand: but surely we will not kill thee. And they bound him with two new cords, and brought him up from the rock.

It is significant to note that although Samson is bound, he came to his next encounter *from* the rock. The Rock of Etam was a natural fortress into the cleft of which Samson had sought refuge. "In this world you will have trouble," Jesus said. "But take heart! I have overcome the world."[125] Sometimes the world finds us even as we are hiding away in the cleft of the rock. But we need not fear, for He has sent the Holy Spirit to comfort us and set us free.

Judges 15:14-15
14 And when he came unto Lehi, the Philistines shouted against him:

---
[125] John 16:33.

*and **the Spirit of the Lord came mightily upon him**, and the cords that were upon his arms became as flax that was **burnt with fire**, and **his bands loosed from off his hands**.* [Emphasis added.]

15 And he found a new jawbone of an ass, and put forth his hand, and took it, and slew a thousand men therewith.

The Spirit burned the restraining ropes wrapped around his wrists. Where the Spirit of the Lord is, there is liberty indeed. The Spirit of fire set Samson free from his bondage and empowered him to cause devastating damage to the enemy's kingdom. The battles we face against principalities, powers, rulers of darkness, and spiritual wickedness require us to be free from the bondage of sin, legalism, and fear to effectively fight the good fight of faith.[126] It is the Spirit's cleansing fire that liberates us to the battlefront.

Consumed by God

We began this chapter with the understanding that our God is a consuming fire. Andrew Murray's insights into this truth are a fitting capstone to our meditation on the Spirit of fire:

> "Fire may be either a blessing or a curse. All depends upon my relation to it whether it meets me as a friend or an enemy. The fire of God, as it comes to purify, to consume the sacrifice and convert it into its own heavenly light-nature, to baptize with the Holy Ghost and with fire, to transform our being into flames of love,— blessed the man who knows His God as a consuming fire. But woe to him on whom the fire of God descends, as on Sodom and Gomorrha, in wrath and judgment. Oh that in the fulness of faith all believers might see and fear this impending judgment, and, moved with the compassion of Christ, give themselves to warn men and

---

[126] Rom. 6:12-15; Gal 5:1-2; Rom. 8:15; Heb. 2:15; 1 Tim. 6:9-12.

snatch them from the fire. **For our God is a consuming fire**."[127]

Let us with holy awe wade into the river of fire in Holy Spirit baptism to have our hearts cleansed, our faith purified, our sacrifice accepted, our bondages burnt, and our works proven that we may receive His full reward, all the while reaching out that others might be saved.

---

[127] Andrew Murray, *The Holiest of All*, Whitaker House, 1996, p. 515-516. Emphasis in original.

CHAPTER 5

Oil

The noble olive and the anointing of God

I grew up in a Christian home of the Baptist persuasion and was in my early teenage years before I encountered the Pentecostal expression of the faith. Even in those first years of learning about the Holy Spirit and His gifts to the saints, I heard little about the significance of oil in Scripture or of its sacramental uses in the church. I am not alone in my experience. I spoke with a teacher from a Christian school recently who writes children's books. One of them is about an oil lamp, and she told me that there was a spirited debate with her pastor and other members of her church when she was writing it as to whether the oil was representative of the Holy Spirit. This is surprising upon reflection, as oil's prevalence in Scripture and its historic use in the Orthodox, Catholic, Anglican, and Lutheran communities—let alone the use of oil in Pentecostal and Charismatic churches—should have made the subject matter obvious.

Acts 10:37-38
37 That word, I say, ye know, which was published throughout all Judaea, and began from Galilee, after the baptism which John preached;
38 How God anointed Jesus of Nazareth with the Holy Ghost and with power: who went about doing good, and healing all that were oppressed of the devil; for God was with him.

"God anointed Jesus of Nazareth with the Holy Ghost" is as strong a reference as one could hope for to establish oil as a symbol for the Holy Spirit. As water is understood to be present in the term "baptism," so oil is understood in the term "anointed." When Scripture speaks of the baptism of the Holy Spirit, water is running through the word picture. What water teaches us about the Holy Spirit should be top of mind. When we read about "the anointing,"[128] it is oil we should contemplate. To anoint is to smear or rub with oil. Peter declared to Cornelius and his household that God smeared Jesus with the Holy Spirit and with power. His statement is a classic example of Hebraic parallelism. To be anointed with the Holy Spirit is to have power rubbed into you.

Jesus the Anointed One

"God anointed *Jesus of Nazareth*." Our Lord's name is Jesus; Christ is His title.[129] "Christ" is the English translation of the Greek term *Christos*, which literally means "one who has been anointed." Messiah means the same thing but comes to us from the Hebrew *meshiyach*.[130] It is the term used for those like priests, prophets, and kings whose consecration to God's service was signified through the anointing ceremony.

Exodus 30:22-25, 30-31
22 Moreover the Lord spoke to Moses, saying:
23 "Also take for yourself quality spices — five hundred shekels of liquid myrrh, half as much sweet-smelling cinnamon (two hundred and fifty shekels), two hundred and fifty shekels of sweet-smelling cane [calamus, Heb. qaneh, Grk. kalamos, a reed, a measuring rod],
24 five hundred shekels of cassia, according to the shekel of the sanctuary, and a hin of olive oil.
25 And you shall make from these a holy anointing oil, an ointment compounded according to the art of the perfumer. It shall be a holy anointing oil.

---

[128] 1 John 2:27.
[129] In particular, when the article *ho*, the, appears before it; the Christ.
[130] See John 1:41.

30 And you shall anoint Aaron and his sons, and consecrate them, that they may minister to Me as priests.

31 "And you shall speak to the children of Israel, saying: 'This shall be a holy anointing oil to Me throughout your generations.' NKJV

As first revealed to Moses, the holy anointing oil was reserved to sanctify the tabernacle and its furnishings, along with the priests that ministered within its confines. Later, this revelation expanded to include kings.

1 Sam 16:13a
Then Samuel took the horn of oil, and anointed him in the midst of his brethren: and the Spirit of the Lord came upon David from that day forward.

Psalm 89:20
I have found David my servant; with my holy oil have I anointed him:

The Gospel of Matthew introduces Jesus Christ as "the son of David, the son of Abraham."[131] Jesus the Messiah, the High Priest after the order of Melchizedek,[132] was descended from David, the anointed king, who was descended from Abraham, the anointed prophet.[133] God preached the good news of Messiah's coming to Abraham when He told him he would be a blessing to all nations.[134] The gospel without the anointing is an incomplete declaration of the work of God. The gospel presented with antagonism to the anointing is anti-Christ, against the Anointed One.[135]

---

[131] Matt. 1:1.

[132] Heb. 6:20.

[133] Gen. 20:3-7; 1 Chron. 16:22; Ps. 105:15.

[134] Gal. 3:8.

[135] I have in mind those who would embrace Jesus as savior yet deny the miraculous works He did and promised His followers would do.

Luke 4:18-19

18 The Spirit of the Lord is upon me, because he hath anointed me to preach the gospel to the poor; he hath sent me to heal the broken-hearted, to preach deliverance to the captives, and recovering of sight to the blind, to set at liberty them that are bruised,
19 To preach the acceptable year of the Lord.

Jesus read these verses, quoted from Isaiah,[136] as His homecoming announcement in the Nazareth synagogue. Their response to this pronouncement was to attempt throwing the Christ off a cliff.[137] The message of the anointing has always been controversial.

John the Baptist declared that God bestowed the Spirit upon Jesus without measure.[138] In contrast, we His followers have only been given a measure of faith.[139] When the Holy Spirit descended upon Jesus as he broke out of Jordan's waters, He came in full anointing—in full presence and empowerment. In Christ dwells the fullness of the Godhead bodily (Col. 1:19). As Jesus in His earthly ministry walked in the complete anointing of the Holy Spirit, so the body of Christ assembled—the Church—should flow in the Spirit's fully anointed work. Isaiah's prophecy and Jesus's declaration tell us how the full anointing of the Holy Spirit is expressed:

- The gospel is preached to the poor. [Salvation]
- The brokenhearted are healed. [Healing]
- Freedom is proclaimed to prisoners. [Deliverance]
- The blind recover their sight. [Revelation]
- The bruised find liberty. [Freedom from iniquity]

---

[136] Isa. 61:1-2a.
[137] Luke 4:21, 28-29.
[138] John 3:34.
[139] Rom. 12:3-8.

The Holy Anointing Oil

The holy anointing oil represents the full anointing of the Holy Spirit. Its ingredients tell the redemption story and signify the five-fold ministry listed above. Jesus died (myrrh) for the world (cinnamon) and received God's judgment (calamus) for man's sin. His sacrifice was a pleasing aroma to God, and we take His fragrance (cassia) to the nations. He is the One who has poured out the Holy Spirit (olive oil, a measure of the anointing) on those who repent and come to Him in faith (Acts 2:33, 38). These truths are correlated in Table 5.1 below.[140]

Ingredient	Symbolizes	Scriptures
Myrrh	Suffering of death	Mark 15:23; John 19:39-40
Cinnamon	Fragrance of the world	Prov. 7:17; Rev. 18:13
Calamus	Judgment	Isa. 46:6; Ezek. 40-42; Rev. 11:1-2
Cassia	Fragrance of Christ	Ps. 45:8; 2 Cor. 2:14-17; Eph. 5:2
Olive Oil	Holy Spirit anointing	Ps. 23:5; Luke 4:17-18; 1 John 2:20, 27

Table 5.1

Gabriel announced to Mary that God would give Jesus the throne of his father David. King David was anointed three times (1 Sam. 16:13; 2 Sam. 2:4; 5:3), and along with being king, he also functioned as a priest (2 Sam. 6:13-18) and a prophet (Acts 2:25-31). Jesus the Anointed One is the Prophet promised through Moses (Deut. 18:15), the high priest over the house of God (Heb. 10:21), and King of kings and Lord of lords (Rev. 19:16). The anointed functions of priest, prophet, and king are aligned with the Holy Spirit's work of the conviction of sin, righteousness, and judgment in our day. Priests offered

---

[140] I owe the insights on the symbolism of the ingredients to Kevin J. Connor, *Interpreting the Symbols and Types: Completely revised and expanded edition*, BT Publishing, Portland, OR, 1992, pp. 27-28, 156, 158. Some correlations are not apparent in English and require original language study helps.

sacrifices for sin, prophets called the people of God to righteousness, and kings executed judgment against those who practiced evil.

Additional biblical truths worthy of consideration regarding the holy anointing oil (HAO) include:

- HAO had five ingredients. Five is the number of grace in Scripture, because numerically it represents the impact of God (1) upon (+) creation (4). We are anointed by the grace of God.[141]
- Though HAO had many aspects, it was one anointing oil. He is one Spirit.[142]
- HAO was prepared in large batches, from which anointings of lesser volume were poured out. In this, we once again see the difference from the anointing we receive and the supplier Himself.
- HAO was used to set people and things apart as holy in service to the Lord.[143]
- HAO was used for generations (Exod. 30:31). The anointing of past generations is insufficient for our consecration. Each generation must be consecrated anew in its own anointing.
- HAO smelled good. The anointed people of God are perfumed with the Holy Spirit.
- The ingredients to make HAO were harvested and made useful through a process of piercing (myrrh), cutting and grinding (cinnamon, calamus, and cassia), and crushing (olive oil). It is because of the suffering and sacrifice of Jesus Christ that we receive the anointing.[144]

---

[141] Zech. 12:10; Titus 3:5-7.
[142] Eph. 4:4.
[143] Exod. 30:25-30.
[144] Acts 2:22-33.

All the aromatic spices were mixed into olive oil, which is a symbol of the Holy Spirit in its own right. Let us now examine what olive oil has to teach us about the Spirit.

Olive Oil, the Medicinal Food

Olive oil brings great flavor to culinary endeavors. But beyond that, it can actually improve one's quality of life. Olive oil is composed mostly of oleic acid, which is a monounsaturated fat. Oleic acid stimulates digestive juice secretion, making it easy to digest, as well as increasing the absorption of nutrients from the foods eaten with it. Olive oil also contains linoleic and linolenic acids in a ratio similar to that found in human milk, which makes it highly suitable for breast-fed and weaned infants.

Olive oil has always held a place somewhere between food and medicine. When the Good Samaritan came across the wounded traveler, he poured oil and wine on the wounds and bandaged him up.[145] Wine has antiseptic qualities. Olive oil is high in vitamin E, which is great for the skin. It is absorbed through the pores without clogging them. Aside from green leafy vegetables like kale and spinach, olive oil is one of the best sources of vitamin K. This nutrient promotes healthy blood clotting ability, keeping our wounds sealed and the blood in our veins flowing. Vitamin K also strengthens our bones and helps prevent their weakening and fracturing.

Olive oil as consumed in a Mediterranean diet has been shown to reduce the risk of breast, prostate, and bowel cancer. The flavonoid polyphenols in olive oil are beneficial in lowering cholesterol, blood pressure and the risk of coronary disease. It helps prevent insulin resistance and ensures better control of glucose in the blood.

---

[145] Luke 10:34.

Who is it that aids our digestion of the Word, keeps our hearts from being hardened, regulates our spiritual energy level, keeps the church from malignant tumorous growths, and is so gentle that His suggestions can be received as easily as mother's milk? The Holy Spirit, of course.

Insights from Organic Chemistry

Olive oil is a complex compound, up to 85% of which is oleic acid. A fatty acid, oleic acid is classified as a monounsaturated fat, because it contains only one carbon double bond along its eighteen-carbon length. A simplified two-dimensional model of this molecule is shown in Figure 5.1 below.

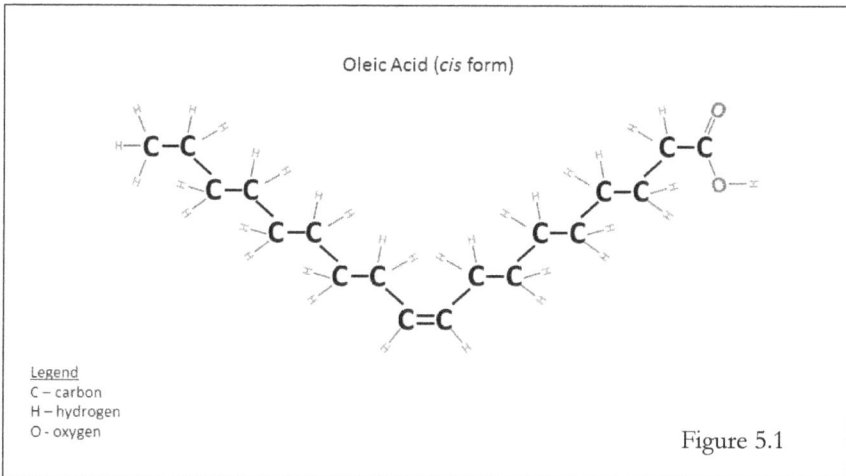

Oleic Acid (*cis* form)

Legend
C – carbon
H – hydrogen
O - oxygen

Figure 5.1

At the right end of this molecule is its carboxylic group (COOH) and is refered to as the "alpha" end of the molecule. At the left side is the methyl end (CH_3) which is referred to as the "omega" end of the molecule. Unsaturated fatty acids are classified by the location of the first carbon double bond from the omega end. Oleic acid is considered an omega-9 fatty acid ,as the double bond occurs at the ninth carbon atom from the omega end. Nine more carbon atoms follow on the other side of the double bond.

What does all this have to do with the Holy Spirit? Nine is a number that is associated with the Holy Spirit in the manifestation gifts (1 Cor. 12:7-12) and the fruit of the Spirit (Gal. 5:22-23).[146] The double bond that kinks the molecule, which helps keep it fluid, gives it a shape that is reminiscent of wings, lending it resonance with two other symbols used for the Holy Spirit in Scripture: the dove and the eagle. Oxygen is contained in the alpha end and speaks to us of Jesus breathing on the disciples to receive the Holy Spirit.[147] The omega end has three hydrogen atoms (all the same, yet three distinct atoms) attached to a carbon atom. This is a picture the Godhead's indwelling of the saint, which is further illustrated by the fact that oleic acid is a triglyceride. It is organized in units of three that attach to one glycerol molecule by their respective carboxyl ends. In this basic unit of the anointing oil, the Creator has left a strong witness of Himself. These truths are summarized in Figures 5.2 and 5.3 below.

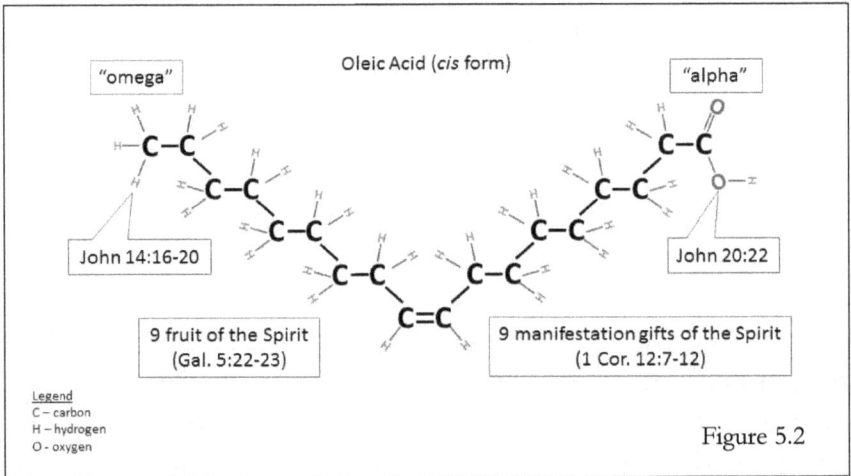

Figure 5.2

---

[146] Jesus "gave up the ghost" in the ninth hour of the day (Luke 23:44-46), making the outpouring of the Holy Spirit possible.
[147] John 20:21-22.

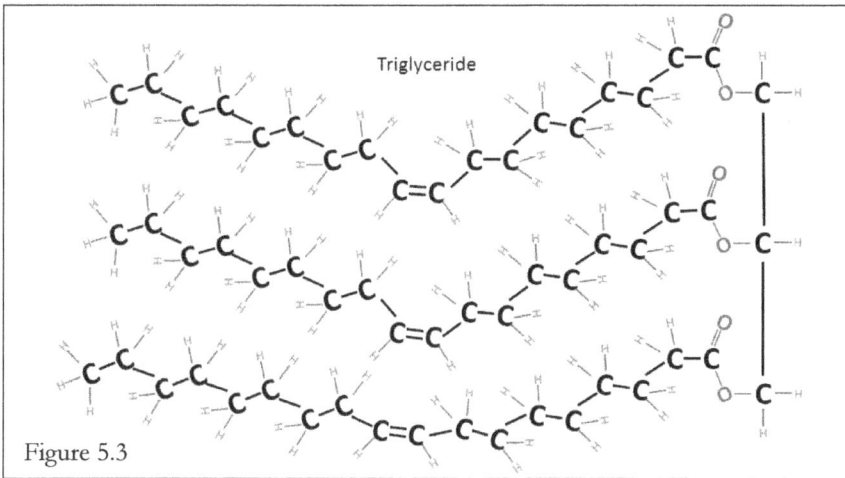
Figure 5.3

The triglyceride structure of oleic acid speaks of the Godhead's working within us in the anointing. As the apostle Paul wrote to the Philippian church, "It is God who works in you to will and do His good pleasure" (Phil. 2:13). Nutritionally, triglycerides are highly concentrated energy stores that contain twice as much energy as carbohydrates or proteins. Like the anointing, they are supercharged. The Spirit's presence in our hearts makes our inner beings mighty.[148]

The Consecration of the Priests

1 Peter 2:9 tells us that we are a "chosen generation, a royal priesthood." This is a quotation of Exodus 19:6, when the Aaronic priesthood was instituted to point toward its ultimate fulfillment.[149] The instructions the Lord gave Moses for the priests' consecration give us insight into what happened to us when we were born again.

Exodus 29:1-3
1 "Now this is what you shall do to them to consecrate them, that they may serve me as priests. Take one bull of the herd and two rams without blemish,

---

[148] Eph. 3:14-16.
[149] "Royal priesthood" speaks of the joining of the offices of king and priest fulfilled by Christ in the Melchizedekian priesthood (Heb. 6-8). It is into this type of priesthood that Christ has brought us to through the redemption of His blood (Rev. 5:9-10).

107

2 and unleavened bread, unleavened cakes mixed with oil, and unleav-
ened wafers smeared with oil. You shall make them of fine wheat
flour.

3 You shall put them in one basket and bring them in the basket, and
bring the bull and the two rams. ESV

The first order of business dealt with in the consecration is the presentation of the sacrifices. Jesus presented himself for sacrifice to the Father in the Garden of Gethsemane. It was there in prayer that he set himself for what was coming. "My Father, if this cup cannot pass away from me unless I drink it, Your will be done," he prayed while sweat dripped like blood from his brow.[150] Gethsemane means "olive press." Olive oil is harvested through the crushing of the olive fruit. In using it as a symbol of Himself throughout Scripture, the Holy Spirit was pointing to the cost of the outpouring. All anointings of the Holy Spirit—past, present, and future—were made possible because Jesus said, "Thy will be done" in the Garden and followed that commitment all the way through the cross.

Note that the sacrifice included a grain offering. Jesus is the bread from heaven broken for us.[151] The cakes were mixed with oil—they had the anointing *within*. The wafers were smeared with oil—they had the anointing *upon*. As with water in washing and drinking,[152] the oil of the Holy Spirit resides in us and falls upon us.

Exodus 29:4-5
4 You shall bring Aaron and his sons to the entrance of the tent of
meeting and wash them with water.

---

[150] Matt. 26:42; Luke 22:44; Heb. 10:5-9. Sweating blood is a condition known as *hematidrosis* and results from burst capillaries around the sweat glands due to severe mental anguish and stress.

[151] John 6:32-35; 12:24; Mark 14:22; 1 Cor. 10:16-17.

[152] This was examined in Chapter 3 under the section heading "Water In and Out."

5 Then you shall take the garments, and put on Aaron the coat and the robe of the ephod, and the ephod, and the breastpiece, and gird him with the skillfully woven band of the ephod. ESV

To wash their bodies, the old clothes—their ordinary, everyday clothes—had to come off. Once cleansed, they were clothed. We saw in Chapter 3 how the washing with water pointed to the baptism of the Holy Spirit. Jesus used the analogy of being clothed in His final instructions to the apostles about the coming of the Holy Spirit.

Luke 24:49
And behold, I am sending the promise of my Father upon you. But stay in the city until you are clothed with power from on high." ESV

Paul used similar language to describe our walk in the newness of Christ.

Ephesians 4:21-24
21 if indeed you have heard Him and have been taught by Him, as the truth is in Jesus:
*22 that **you put off**, concerning your former conduct, the old man which grows corrupt according to the deceitful lusts,*
23 and be renewed in the spirit of your mind,
*24 and that **you put** on the new man which was created according to God, in true righteousness and holiness. NKJV* [Emphasis added.]

Once clothed, Aaron and his sons had the blood of the sacrifice and the anointing oil spattered on them.

Exodus 29:21
Then you shall take part of the blood that is on the altar, and of the anointing oil, and sprinkle [Hebrew *nazah*, to spatter or sprinkle with the finger or a sprinkler] *it on Aaron and his garments, and on his sons and his sons' garments with him. He and his garments shall be holy, and his sons and his sons' garments with him. ESV*

The garments for Aaron and his sons were expertly woven and made "for glory and for beauty."[153] Their coats were made of fine linen, white and clean. Once the priests were arrayed in these beautiful clothes, blood and oil were spattered on them. These were not stains to be laundered out. They were marks of consecration, symbols of the sacrifice that cleansed them and the Spirit that empowered them to mediate between God and man. Even as the priests in the tabernacle were sprinkled with blood and anointed with oil, we have been cleansed by the blood of Jesus Christ and anointed by God with the Holy Spirit.

2 Corinthians 1:21-22
21 Now He who establishes us with you in Christ and has anointed us
   is God,
22 who also has sealed us and given us the Spirit in our hearts as a
   guarantee. NKJV

The rite of priestly consecration had many components that composed one ceremony. This understanding can help us appreciate the different aspects of the new birth. A commonly held belief in many Charismatic and Pentecostal circles is the idea that receiving "the anointing"—the baptism of the Holy Spirit—is a subsequent act of grace *after* being born again. Personally, I do not see it that way, even though many people experience it that way.

In the process of their consecration, the priests were washed, clothed, bloodied, and anointed. When we were born again by the grace of God, we became His people and priests in His kingdom. The blood of Jesus redeemed us, and the Holy Spirit washed, clothed, and anointed us.[154] Though we may discover the impact and significance of these realities at different times, they are all part of us being a new creation in Christ. Those who have believed in Jesus are born of God, and the

---

[153] Exod. 28:39-41.
[154] Rev. 5:9-10; Titus 3:4-7; Gal. 3:13-14, 26-27; 1 John 2:20, 27.

Spirit bears witness to this truth, crying "Abba, Father!" in our hearts.[155] To be born again is to receive the anointing of the Holy Spirit within our spirit.

Oil Soaks In

Psalm 109 offers us another glimpse of the qualitative differences between being clothed, anointed, and watered. In this case, it involves a curse—specifically a prophetic curse written about Judas Iscariot—but the truth applies to the blessing of the Holy Spirit as well.

Psalm 109:17-19
17 As he loved cursing, so let it come unto him: as he delighted not in blessing, so let it be far from him.
*18 As he **clothed himself** with cursing like as with his garment, so let it come into his **bowels like water**, and **like oil into his bones**.*
19 Let it be unto him as the garment which covereth him, and for a girdle wherewith he is girded continually. [Emphasis added.]

He clothed himself with cursing. Jesus became a curse for us that we might receive the blessings of Abraham, the promise of the Spirit (Gal. 3:13-14). To walk in this blessing we have received, we need to put off the old man and put on the new man that is created in Christ. We are enjoined to put on the armor of light, the Lord Jesus Christ (Rom. 13:12-14). Our girdle is to be truth not cursing, and we are to be arrayed in the full armor of God (Eph. 6:10-18).

Note in verse 18 that water comes into the bowels and oil soaks into the bones. Water is a washer and a solvent. It helps carry things off and through. Olive oil is a food, medicine, and cosmetic all rolled up into one. It brings things in. Recent studies have shown that consumption of olive oil increases the presence of osteocalcin in human

---

[155] John 1:12-13; Rom. 8:15-16.

blood.[156] Osteocalcin is a bone matrix protein that acts as a hormone in the body, aiding in bone mineralization and calcium ion homeostasis. It builds bones.

When the Holy Spirit interacts with us like water, He is cleansing and refreshing us while making us a spring for others. When He relates to us like oil, He infuses us with His essence and builds strength in our spiritual framework. As His oil soaks in, it perfumes us with the sweet and fruity fragrance of love, joy, peace, longsuffering, gentleness, goodness, faith, meekness, and self-control. It is His anointing that breaks us from the yoke of the flesh.

Galatians 5:16
This I say then, Walk in the Spirit, and ye shall not fulfil the lust of the flesh.

Isaiah 10:27
It shall come to pass in that day That his burden will be taken away from your shoulder, And his yoke from your neck, And the yoke will be destroyed because of the anointing oil. NKJV

Oil, Healing, and the Holy Spirit
Though anointing the sick with oil may be a staple of Pentecostal ministry, it is a practice for the entire church of Christ.

---

[156] José Manuel Fernández-Real and others, "A Mediterranean Diet Enriched with Olive Oil is Associated with Higher Serum Total Osteocalcin Levels in Elderly Men at High Cardiovascular Risk." *The Journal of Clinical Endocrinology & Metabolism*, Volume 97, Issue 10, 1 October 2012, Pages 3792–3798, https://academic.oup.com/jcem/article-lookup/doi/10.1210/jc.2012-2221 (accessed August 20, 2017) and Chin, Kok-Yong, and Soelaiman Ima-Nirwana. "Olives and Bone: A Green Osteoporosis Prevention Option." Ed. Paul B. Tchounwou. *International Journal of Environmental Research and Public Health* 13.8 (2016):755, https://www.ncbi.nlm.nih.gov/pmc/articles/PMC4997441/ (accessed August 20, 2018).

James 5:14-15

14 Is any sick among you? let him call for the elders of the church; and let them pray over him, anointing him with oil in the name of the Lord:

15 And the prayer of faith shall save the sick, and the Lord shall raise him up; and if he have committed sins, they shall be forgiven him.

The most detailed anointing for healing in the Law is the ceremony for the cleansing of the leper found in Leviticus 14. Once a leper was cleansed of his disease, he was to present himself for examination to the priest. We see Jesus instructing lepers to do just that.[157] In the second stage of the cleansing ceremony, the person being declared clean is anointed with oil.

Leviticus 14:14-18

14 And the priest shall take some of the blood of the trespass offering, and the priest shall put it upon the tip of the right ear of him that is to be cleansed, and upon the thumb of his right hand, and upon the great toe of his right foot:

15 And the priest shall take some of the log of oil, and pour it into the palm of his own left hand:

16 And the priest shall dip his right finger in the oil that is in his left hand, and shall sprinkle of the oil with his finger seven times before the Lord:

17 And of the rest of the oil that is in his hand shall the priest put upon the tip of the right ear of him that is to be cleansed, and upon the thumb of his right hand, and upon the great toe of his right foot, upon the blood of the trespass offering:

18 And the remnant of the oil that is in the priest's hand he shall pour upon the head of him that is to be cleansed: and the priest shall make an atonement for him before the Lord.

---

[157] Luke 17:12-14; Matt. 8:2-4.

In light of these verses, James's proclamation that the person healed receives forgiveness of sins is not surprising. Healing is a manifestation of forgiveness.[158] The cleansed leper had the blood of the sacrifice applied to his right ear, right thumb, and right big toe. After being sprinkled seven times on the altar of burnt offering, the oil was applied over the blood and then poured on the head of the one being cleansed. Taken all together, these Scriptures bring us some startling truths.

James tells the elders to anoint the sick with oil and pray in faith for the sick *to be* restored. In Luke, Jesus told the lepers to show themselves to the priests and they were cleansed *as they went*. The anointing in Leviticus 14 is for those who were *already well*—they no longer had leprosy—to be declared cleansed. When we anoint the sick with oil, we are saying "You *are* healed." It is a symbolic act of faith reminding all involved of the accomplished work of Jesus Christ. Earlier we saw that while water washes thing out, oil brings things in. What is the oil bringing into the cleansed leper? The blood of the sacrifice. In like manner, the Holy Spirit brings into us the reality of Jesus's cleansing blood that bought forgiveness and healing for us on the cross.

Food, medicine, and ointment were not the only uses of olive oil in Scripture. Oil was also used as a fuel source for the golden lampstand. It is to this symbol we turn to next.

---

[158] Matt. 9:4-6.

CHAPTER 6

Lamp

The golden lampstand in the holy place

We have seen the Holy Spirit as fire and as the anointing oil. The lamp combines these symbols and provides us with new insights into the Spirit's character. When oil catches flame, we have a lamp. In His first appearance as a lamp, the Holy Spirit showed Himself as a covenant-making and covenant-keeping God.

Genesis 15:9-10, 17-18

9 And he said unto him, Take me an heifer of three years old, and a she goat of three years old, and a ram of three years old, and a tur-tledove, and a young pigeon.

10 And he took unto him all these, and divided them in the midst, and laid each piece one against another: but the birds divided he not.

*17 And it came to pass, that, when the sun went down, and it was dark, behold a smoking furnace, and **a burning lamp that passed between those pieces.***

*18 In the same day **the Lord made a covenant with Abram** ...* [Emphasis added.]

As a light in the darkness, the Holy Spirit walks in the blood of the sacrifice, showing His commitment to the covenant He made with Himself.[159] God's unilateral covenant with Abraham carried Him all the way through the cross to pour out upon us the blessing of the Spir-

---

[159] Heb. 6:13.

it.[160] The Lord's walk in the darkness in the face of Abraham's weakness shows us that His promises come to us through His Spirit, not our strength.

Zechariah 4:1-6

1 Now the angel who talked with me came back and wakened me, as a man who is wakened out of his sleep.

2 And he said to me, "What do you see?" So I said, "I am looking, and there is a lampstand of solid gold with a bowl on top of it, and on the stand seven lamps with seven pipes to the seven lamps.

3 Two olive trees are by it, one at the right of the bowl and the other at its left."

4 So I answered and spoke to the angel who talked with me, saying, "What are these, my lord?"

5 Then the angel who talked with me answered and said to me, "Do you not know what these are?" And I said, "No, my lord."

6 So he answered and said to me: "This is the word of the Lord to Zerubbabel: 'Not by might nor by power, but by My Spirit,' Says the Lord of hosts. NKJV

The Lord gives us great instruction in walking by the Spirit in this narrative. Note how God is communicating with the prophet. He didn't roll him out of bed and shout, "Overcome by my Spirit!" He sent an angel alarm and asked, "What do you see?" Expressing and communicating are not the same thing. God is intent on communication. He gave Zechariah a vision and then asked for verification of what was being seen. The prophet dutifully described what was before his spiritual eyes and then asked, "What are these?" When we receive a vision, it would do us well to ask the meaning of it instead of assuming. "This is a picture of my Spirit," the Lord told him.

Seven is a scripturally pregnant number. God rested on the seventh day and blessed it. Seven is the combination of the divine (three) with

---

[160] Gal. 3:13-14.

creation (four) showing God's connection to the earth in mercy and grace. This grace and mercy is brought to earth by His Spirit and, as such, seven speaks of the perfect completeness of the Spirit.

Isaiah 11:1-2
1 And there shall come forth a rod out of the stem of Jesse, and a Branch shall grow out of his roots:
2 And the spirit of the Lord [1] shall rest upon him, the spirit of wisdom [2] and understanding [3], the spirit of counsel [4] and might [5], the spirit of knowledge [6] and of the fear of the Lord;[7] [Numbers and brackets added.]

We have already seen that Jesus was anointed with the full measure of the Holy Spirit. This prophecy in Isaiah identifies the aspects of the sevenfold Spirit of God. The Holy Spirit chose the symbol of the lampstand to represent Himself to mankind. The revelation that Moses received concerning the tabernacle comes to full light in the vison given to the apostle John.

Revelation 1:4-6
4 John to the seven churches which are in Asia: Grace be unto you, and peace, from him which is, and which was, and which is to come; and from the seven Spirits which are before his throne;
5 And from Jesus Christ, who is the faithful witness, and the first begotten of the dead, and the prince of the kings of the earth. Unto him that loved us, and washed us from our sins in his own blood,
6 And hath made us kings and priests unto God and his Father; to him be glory and dominion for ever and ever. Amen.

The entire Godhead addresses the seven churches in Asia. "From him which is, and which was, and which is to come" is the Father, YHWH. "From Jesus Christ" is clearly the Son. "From the seven Spirits which are before his throne" is the sevenfold Spirit of God.

Revelation 4:5
Out from the throne came flashes of lightning and rumblings and peals
of thunder, and in front of the throne seven blazing torches burned,
which are the seven Spirits of God [the sevenfold Holy Spirit]; AMP

The Lessons in the Lampstand

Moses was instructed to build the tabernacle "according to the pattern"
because it was a representation of God's throne room in heaven.[161]
Brought up to heaven by the Spirit, John witnessed the reality of
which the holy place and holy of holies were only a shadow. There
before the throne flamed the Holy Spirit in glorious golden lampstand
form. Few of us travel there in this life. Thankfully, the testimony of
the lampstand in the tabernacle is open to all.

Exodus 25:31-32
31 "You shall also make a lampstand of pure gold; the lampstand shall
*   be of hammered work. Its shaft, its branches, its bowls, its orna-*
*   mental knobs, and flowers shall be of one piece.*
32 And six branches shall come out of its sides: three branches of the
*   lampstand out of one side, and three branches of the lampstand*
*   out of the other side. NKJV*

The lampstand was made of pure gold. He is the *Holy* Spirit; no impurities are found in Him. Pure gold is what we refer to as 24-karat gold.
A karat is 1/24 part of pure gold by weight. Most gold jewelry is al-
loyed with other metals to provide it with greater firmness, since gold
is very malleable. It can be hammered or pressed out of shape without
breaking or cracking. One ounce of gold can be beaten out to 300
square feet. The oil for the lamp was *pure oil* pressed out of olives for
light.[162] As the olives were pressed and crushed, the gold was hammered *without breaking*.

---

[161] Heb. 8:5.
[162] Lev. 24:2.

John 19:32-33, 36

32 Then came the soldiers, and brake the legs of the first, and of the other which was crucified with him.

33 But when they came to Jesus, and saw that he was dead already, they brake not his legs:

*36 For these things were done, that the scripture should be fulfilled, **A bone of him shall not be broken.*** [Emphasis added.]

The Holy Spirit bears witness of Jesus Christ.[163] The oil press and the goldsmith's hammer tell us of the sacrifice of our Lord, so that the promised Holy Spirit could come. The lampstand had a central column with three branches on either side providing seven total stands for the lamps. Man was made on the sixth day. As such, six is the number of man in Scripture.[164] Jesus was the one sacrifice for all mankind.[165] In the shape of the lampstand, we have an allusion to the cross as well as a reference to the image of the vine and the branches.[166] As the Father prunes the branches, so Jesus our High Priest trims the wicks of the lamp.[167]

Exodus 25:33-36

33 Three bowls shall be made like almond blossoms on one branch, with an ornamental knob and a flower, and three bowls made like almond blossoms on the other branch, with an ornamental knob and a flower — and so for the six branches that come out of the lampstand.

34 On the lampstand itself four bowls shall be made like almond blossoms, each with its ornamental knob and flower.

35 And there shall be a knob under the first two branches of the same, a knob under the second two branches of the same, and a knob un-

---

[163] John 16:13-14; Rev. 19:10.
[164] Gen. 1:26-32; Rev. 13:18.
[165] Rom. 5:12-21; Heb. 9:27-28; 10:12.
[166] John 15:1-5.
[167] Rev. 1:12-13.

der the third two branches of the same, according to the six branches that extend from the lampstand.

36 Their knobs and their branches shall be of one piece; all of it shall be one hammered piece of pure gold.

The lampstand was crafted in an almond tree motif. The Hebrew word translated "almond" is *shaqed* and means "the waker" because it blooms as early as January or February when all the other trees are still in their winter's sleep. As such, it is a symbol of resurrection. When the children of Israel doubted Aaron's appointment as high priest, Moses asked each of the tribal leaders to bring their staffs and place them before the Lord in the tabernacle. These staffs or rods were dry, dead branches. But the next morning, Aaron's dead almond tree rod was found to have sprouted, budded, bloomed, and produced almonds.[168]

Each branch of the lampstand had three sets of a bud, flower, and almond ornament. Three times three is nine, and as we saw when we examined the anointing oil, nine speaks of the manifestation gifts of the Spirit[169] as well as the nine fruit of the Spirit.[170]

The Purpose of the Lamps
Exodus 25:37
*You shall make seven lamps for it, and they shall arrange its lamps **so that they give light in front of it.** NKJV* [Emphasis added.]

The tabernacle was a tent formed with four layers of fabric: linen, wool, ram's skin, and porpoise hide. A thick cloth door closed the holy place off from the courtyard. Seven oil lamps were all that lit the room the priests performed their daily functions in. We have all lived our lives bathed in electric lighting. On rare occasions when the power goes out, we may break out the candles and the lamps to make do. I

---

[168] Num. 17:1-8.
[169] 1 Cor. 12:7-11.
[170] Gal. 5:22-23.

have tried reading by candlelight. It is not an easy task. If you envision the holy place being dim, it is only because you have forgotten the gold. Gold is 95% reflective. All the furniture in the holy place—the lampstand, the table of showbread, and the altar of incense—was made with gold. The boards that formed the walls were all overlaid in gold. As the lamps burned, their light bounced back and forth among the gold surfaces, bathing the entire space in a glorious glow.

The lamps were arranged "so that they give light in front of it." What sat on the other side of the lampstand was the table of showbread. Though the light of the lamps lit the room and all its furnishings, its primary purpose was to illuminate the table of showbread. This showbread, or the bread of the Presence, was representative of the bread from heaven, the Lord Jesus Christ, whose body was broken for us.[171] Once again we see the Spirit's humbleness in that He speaks not of Himself but of Jesus Christ (John 16:13-14). This testimony has a second witness in the veil, which shimmered in the lamplight and represented the flesh of Christ.[172]

The bread also speaks of the word of God, for "man shall not live by bread alone, but by every word that proceeds from the mouth of God."[173] Since it was the Holy Spirit who inspired the writing of Scripture,[174] it is He who must give us an understanding of it.

1 Corinthians 2:12-14
12 Now we have received, not the spirit of the world, but the spirit which is of God; that we might know the things that are freely given to us of God.
13 Which things also we speak, not in the words which man's wisdom teacheth, but which the Holy Ghost teacheth; comparing spiritual things with spiritual.

---

[171] 1 Cor. 11:23-24.
[172] Heb. 10:20.
[173] Matt. 4:4.
[174] 2 Pet. 2:21; 2 Tim. 3:16-17.

14 But the natural man receiveth not the things of the Spirit of God: for they are foolishness unto him: neither can he know them, because they are spiritually discerned.

The truth of Scripture must be illuminated by the Spirit's holy light. It cannot be grasped with human intellect alone. Bible students without the Spirit have facts and knowledge, but not truth. The Holy Spirit is the Spirit of truth and the revealer of it. As A. W. Tozer states, "To understand the Bible text takes an act of the Holy Spirit equal to the act that inspired it in the first place."[175]

A great example of this is in the building of the tabernacle itself. For a fun, practical exercise in seeing this principle in action, gather a group of people together and give them all pencils and sketch pads. Have them read Exodus 25 and ask them to sketch out the ark of the covenant, the table of showbread, and the golden lampstand. My guess is that at the end of the exercise you will have as many different illustrations as there are artists. Though the Scripture gives us a good idea of the materials and dimensions of these furnishings, we cannot envision exactly what they are supposed to look like.

Exodus 31:1-8
1 Then the Lord spoke to Moses, saying:
2 "See, I have called by name Bezalel the son of Uri, the son of Hur, of the tribe of Judah.
*3 And **I have filled him with the Spirit of God**, in wisdom, in understanding, in knowledge, and in all manner of workmanship,*
4 to design artistic works, to work in gold, in silver, in bronze,
5 in cutting jewels for setting, in carving wood, and to work in all manner of workmanship.
6 "And I, indeed I, have appointed with him Aholiab the son of Ahisamach, of the tribe of Dan; and I have put wisdom in the hearts

---

[175] A. W. Tozer, *The Counselor: Straight Talk about the Holy Spirit from a 20th-Century Prophet* (Christian Publications, Inc., 1993), 24.

*of all the gifted artisans, **that they may make all that I have commanded you:***

7 the tabernacle of meeting, the ark of the Testimony and the mercy seat that is on it, and all the furniture of the tabernacle —

8 the table and its utensils, the pure gold lampstand with all its utensils, the altar of incense, NKJV [Emphasis added.]

"Make sure you stick to the pattern I showed you on the mountain," the Lord warned Moses as the prophet started the tabernacle building project.[176] The Holy Spirit inspired him to write down the general directions. But to actually build it to exact specifications—with clear understanding of the directions and the truthfulness of the design—required men anointed with the Spirit of God. The Spirit revealed to them the true meaning of the words and enabled them to carry it out. It is no different with us. We can read verses about renewing our minds, loving our enemies, or having faith in Christ. But absent the Holy Spirit's light in our hearts regarding those words, we remain devoid of true understanding or the power to change.

The incense smoke from the golden altar in the holy place symbolized prayer and worship rising to God in heaven.[177] Though this piece of furniture had its own light source, the burning incense, it was not left to function in the dim red glow of its own embers. The lampstand provided the external illumination necessary to carry out the incense ministry correctly and revealed the rising smoke in all its turbulent beauty. "God is Spirit," Jesus told the woman at the well, and "those who worship Him must worship Him in spirit and in truth."[178] Even as the lampstand gave its light to the priests ministering to the Lord through the altar of incense, the Spirit leads us in true worship.

---

[176] Heb. 8:5.
[177] Ps. 141:2; Isa. 6:1-4; Rev. 5:8-9.
[178] John 4:24.

Ephesians 5:18-20

*18 And be not drunk with wine, wherein is excess; but **be filled with the Spirit**;*

*19 Speaking to yourselves in psalms and hymns and **spiritual songs**, singing and making melody in your heart to the Lord;*

20 Giving thanks always for all things unto God and the Father in the name of our Lord Jesus Christ; [Emphasis added.]

Romans 8:26

Likewise the Spirit also helpeth our infirmities: for we know not what we should pray for as we ought: but the Spirit itself maketh intercession for us with groanings which cannot be uttered.

The lampstand's light also revealed the lampstand itself. The Spirit does make Himself known to us. But this work is incidental in His greater mission to bear testimony to Jesus and convict the world of sin, righteousness, and judgment.

Lights for Battle

Born-again saints are birthed on a battlefield. What the Lord revealed to Zechariah is just as true for us. The enemies we fight are not flesh and blood. We cannot overcome spiritual enemies with our own might and power. We must do so by the Spirit.

Ephesians 6:10-11

10 Finally, my brethren, be strong in the Lord, and in the power of his might.

11 Put on the whole armour of God, that ye may be able to stand against the wiles of the devil.

Regarding the arrangement of the lamps, we read following in Exodus:

Exodus 39:37

*the pure gold lampstand with its lamps **(the lamps set in order)**, all its utensils, and the oil for light; NKJV* [Emphasis added.]

The Hebrew word translated "set in order" is *ma'arakah*, and it means "to arrange in a battle-line." The idea is that of setting an army in array. All the lamps were lined up facing forward. Through His revelatory work in words of knowledge, words of wisdom, and discerning of spirits, the Holy Spirit directs us into battle against the enemy, for though we walk in the flesh, we do not war after the flesh.[179]

2 Samuel 22:29-30
29 For thou art my lamp, O Lord: and the Lord will lighten my darkness.
30 For by thee I have run through a troop: by my God have I leaped over a wall.

The Lampstand and the High Priest
Leviticus 24:2-4
*2 "Command the Israelites to bring you clear oil of pressed olives for the light so that the lamps may be **kept burning continually**.*
*3 Outside the curtain of the Testimony in the Tent of Meeting, Aaron is to **tend the lamps** before the Lord from evening till morning, **continually**. This is to be a lasting ordinance for the generations to come.*
*4 The lamps on the pure gold lampstand before the Lord **must be tended continually**. NIV* [Emphasis added.]

Oil lamps require tending to keep burning. In the case of the tabernacle, this was a daily duty. The lamps had to be filled with oil, and the wicks needed to be trimmed. Untrimmed wicks produce smoke—evidence of an unclean burning. If the oil runs out, the lamp's light dies. In the ministry of the lampstand, the Holy Spirit instructs us in the attentiveness of Jesus toward His church and the need of the church to remain in relationship with—in the flow of—the Spirit. Resisting Him or grieving Him is tantamount to pushing away His fresh supply of oil in our lives. Refusing the trimming shears is to press

---

[179] 2 Cor. 10:3-4.

forward presumptuously in the inclinations of our burned-out flesh, obscuring our witnesses and poisoning the atmosphere of our outreach.

Note the stress on continuity in the verses above. No relationship should be taken for granted, least of all our relationship with the Holy Spirit. Like our daily bread, we require fresh oil for new light *every day*. If we neglect this duty, our view of the truth is sure to become obscured through smoke and darkness. Things we once saw clearly and believed, we begin to wonder at and doubt. But when we remain attached to the Vine and the High Priest of our confession and determine to be pliant under the Spirit's convicting hand, the fresh flow of His Holy Oil burns with pure light, showing us the way to walk in His grace.

Revelation 1:12-13
12 Then I turned to see the voice that spoke with me. And having turned I saw seven golden lampstands,
13 and in the midst of the seven lampstands One like the Son of Man, clothed with a garment down to the feet and girded about the chest with a golden band. NKJV

John saw Jesus in the midst of the lampstands in the heavenly tabernacle. As our High Priest, He oils the lamps and trims the wicks. Peter declared on the day of Pentecost that it was Jesus who had "poured out" the promised Holy Spirit.[180] As we will see in the parable of the virgins, it is through our *continual* relationship with Him that the flow of the Spirit is maintained.

Matthew 12:20
*A bruised reed he will not break, and **a smoldering wick he will not snuff out**, till he leads justice to victory. NIV [Emphasis added.]*

---

[180] Acts 2:32-33.

Jesus is in the business of oiling lamps and trimming wicks so that they remain vibrant and bright. When we are weak and burned out, He lovingly trims away the charred portions of our lives and graciously pours out fresh oil to revive us.

The Lampstand and the Church
Revelation 1:20
The mystery of the seven stars which you saw in My right hand, and the seven golden lampstands: The seven stars are the angels of the seven churches, and the seven lampstands which you saw are the seven churches. NKJV

The lampstand is not only representative of the Holy Spirit but also a symbol of the church itself. This makes absolute sense. As image bearers of the Creator and temples of the Holy Spirit, it stands to reason that we should reflect His nature.[181] The purpose of a lampstand is to provide a place for the lamp *to stand*. Christianity is not a calling to hermitic religion but the placement within the relational covenant community of the Godhead. As we are intended to be members of the body—and thus attached to it—so we are called to shine our lights from the lampstand.

Matthew 5:14-16
14 "You are the light of the world. A city that is set on a hill cannot be hidden.
15 Nor do they light a lamp and put it under a basket, but on a lampstand, and it gives light to all who are in the house.
16 Let your light so shine before men, that they may see your good works and glorify your Father in heaven. NKJV

The Christian faith needs to be walked out in the community of the church. It is when we are on a lampstand that our light shines to all in the house, exposing our good works and bringing glory to our Father.

---

[181] 2 Cor. 3:18.

It is love that brings this about. For love to be love, it must be shared; otherwise it is just secret desire concealed in fear.

Luke 11:33
"No one, when he has lit a lamp, puts it in a secret place or under a basket, but on a lampstand, that those who come in may see the light. NKJV

As Jeremiah found out, when we try to bottle up the light of God in our weak clay vessels, we only manage to burn our bones down to ash.[182] Love is expressed in community. When we neglect love, we stand in danger of losing our relationships.

Revelation 2:4-5
4 Nevertheless I have this against you, that you have left your first love.
5 Remember therefore from where you have fallen; repent and do the first works, or else I will come to you quickly and remove your lampstand from its place — unless you repent. NKJV

As the High Priest among the lampstands, Jesus put the church of Ephesus on notice: no work took precedence over their need to love Him. He will not bear with a church that does not love Him. Like a husband whose wife is dutiful but not devoted, He is unsatisfied with a relationship devoid of passion. The price of His displeasure is high. Unrepentant, we could find ourselves scattered about the floor, fallen beneath bushels and beds and locked out of the wedding feast.

The Lamps of the Ten Virgins
The parable of the ten virgins is found in Matthew 25:1-13. In sermons and teachings, it is common to contrast the five wise virgins with the five foolish ones. Though this is unavoidable as it is exactly what Je-

---

[182] Jer. 20:7-9; 2 Cor. 4:6-7.

sus is doing in the parable, it is also useful for us to recognize what the Master said the virgins had in common.

- They were all pure (virgins).
- They all had lamps.
- They all became drowsy and fell asleep while waiting for the bridegroom.
- They all woke up at the announcement of the bridegroom's arrival.
- They all trimmed their lamps.

Thus far, there are no differences in these two groups. All ten women are commendable. They have maintained their purity. They walk in the light. They are spiritually responsive to their Lord's call. They responsibly tend to their wicks. The only potential criticism to all ten of them is that they fell asleep. Our Lord calls us to be ever vigilant, awake and watchful for His return.[183] We should take note that even wise virgins are in danger of growing weary and falling asleep. Sleepers can awaken, but only the well-oiled ones can continue to shine.

Matthew 25:1-4
1 Then shall the kingdom of heaven be likened unto ten virgins, which
 took their lamps, and went forth to meet the bridegroom.
2 And five of them were wise, and five were foolish.
3 They that were foolish took their lamps, and took no oil with them:
4 But the wise took oil in their vessels with their lamps.

What differentiated five of the virgins as wise was their extra supply of oil. We can be attentive to all of our Christian disciplines, but if we run out of oil, we fall to foolishness. As we read in Isaiah, the Holy Spirit is the Spirit of wisdom. Without Him, we become limited to our own human understanding, which is by definition foolish.

---

[183] Luke 12:37-40; 1 Thess. 5:6; Rom. 13:11-12; Eph. 5:14.

Matthew 25:8-10

8 And the foolish said unto the wise, Give us of your oil; for our lamps are gone out.

9 But the wise answered, saying, Not so; lest there be not enough for us and you: but go ye rather to them that sell, and buy for yourselves.

10 And while they went to buy, the bridegroom came; and they that were ready went in with him to the marriage: and the door was shut.

The Holy Spirit's work in us as fuel for enlightenment is different than His flow through us in the anointing. When Moses became overwhelmed with his responsibility of leading the children of Israel, the Lord took of the Spirit that was on him (his anointing to lead) and distributed it among the seventy elders.[184] Elisha received a double portion of Elijah's anointing.[185] When we minister the Spirit to people, we are sharing the anointing. As the lamp, the Holy Spirit does not function this way. The purpose of the oil is to set each of us aflame so that we can shine His goodness on all. It is the *light* that is shared, not the *oil*. Each must have his own oil or risk facing a shut door.

Matthew 25:11-13

11 Afterward came also the other virgins, saying, Lord, Lord, open to us.

12 But he answered and said, Verily I say unto you, I know you not.

13 Watch therefore, for ye know neither the day nor the hour wherein the Son of man cometh.

The Lord's admonition at the end of the parable is for us to remain watchful so that His arrival does not find us unprepared. Though the wise virgins fell asleep, they took enough care to have extra. It was their strength that ran out, not the oil. The foolish virgins attempted to

---

[184] Num. 11:11-17.
[185] 2 Kings 2:9-15.

run on the power of their wicks. When we burn without the oil of the Spirit, we burn out. How do we stay supplied? We need to remain in relationship with the Bridegroom. It requires loving communication.

Mark 14:37-38
37 And he cometh, and findeth them sleeping, and saith unto Peter, Simon, sleepest thou? couldest not thou watch one hour?
38 Watch ye and pray, lest ye enter into temptation. The spirit truly is ready, but the flesh is weak.

Watchfulness requires engaging our spirit in prayer. Prayer is communion with our God. It is impossible to maintain a relationship without communication. For love to be love, it must be shared. Our God is love because the Godhead is an eternal love relationship of the Persons. "I know you not" gives us the seriousness of what it means to run out of oil, to depart from the love of the Spirit. It was because of their forsaking of their first love that the Ephesians faced the prospect of having their lampstand removed.[186] Jesus speaks to the church in Sardis as He who has "the seven Spirits of God"[187] (which John saw as seven lamps before the throne)[188] and calls them to watchfulness lest their names be blotted out of the book of life.[189] If we fail to watch—if we let our lamps run dry and burn out—we risk hearing the worst words anyone could ever hear Jesus utter, "I do not know you."

The Greek word translated "know" in Matthew 25:12 is the word *oida* and speaks of the relationship of the object with the knower. The Lord's declaration here is essentially "you stand in no relation to me." Entrance into the wedding feast of the Lamb requires the bride to be in loving relationship with the Bridegroom. It means that we have remained devoted to Him and unspotted by the world.[190]

---

[186] Rev. 2:4-5.
[187] Rev. 3:1.
[188] Rev. 4:5.
[189] Rev 3:2-6.
[190] 2 Cor. 11:2.

Revelation 19:7-9

7 Let us be glad and rejoice, and give honour to him: for the marriage of the Lamb is come, and his wife hath made herself ready.

8 And to her was granted that she should be arrayed in fine linen, clean and white: for the fine linen is the righteousness of saints.

9 And he saith unto me, Write, Blessed are they which are called unto the marriage supper of the Lamb. And he saith unto me, These are the true sayings of God.

"His wife hath made herself ready." Grace espoused us to Him, and devoted discipleship will wed us to Him. Love is the oil for the light that will see us all the way to the end.

1 Corinthians 16:22

If anyone does not love the Lord [does not have a friendly affection for Him and is not kindly disposed toward Him], he shall be accursed! Our Lord will come! (Maranatha!) AMP

Being cursed at the Lord's return is not the vision of the hope I hold, but it is a possibility I face if I forsake my first love. Emotional divorcement is the rejection of our former object of affection. We turn cold when we turn away. We no longer care about their concerns, desires, or demands. We have selfishly embraced our own agendas to the exclusion of their claim on our hearts. Thankfully, God has frontloaded the relationship in our favor. We love Him because He *first* loved us—He took the initiative in sending the Son to save us. Jesus loved us and gave Himself for us, forever showing what it really means to be a loving husband.[191] After ascending to heaven, Jesus sent the Holy Spirit to us so that we would be able to reciprocate His love.

Romans 5:5

And hope maketh not ashamed; because the love of God is shed abroad in our hearts by the Holy Ghost which is given unto us.

---

[191] Gal. 2:20; Eph. 5:25-33.

Love makes hope shameless. Pride and hypocrisy shut off the supply of love oil in our lives. To express love at the level of the Godhead requires their oil. We are not naturally predisposed to bless those who curse us and pray for those who evilly treat us. We are not inclined to give our lives to save those who not only are ungrateful for the sacrifice but are also acting participants in our slaughter. That being said, there are those who, seeing a need, decide to meet it in their own strength—even if they lack the resource—for the primary benefit of improving their own self-image. These are foolish lamps that offer only their dry wicks to the flame.

1 Corinthians 13:3
And though I bestow all my goods to feed the poor, and though I give my body to be burned, but have not love, it profits me nothing. NKJV

Burning without love brings no profit. It is to burn as a candle—by self-consumption—instead of as a lamp, which burns the Spirit's supply. If the love we share is the Holy Spirit's own, He will continue to pour into us. If we operate from the flesh or close our hearts to charity, we will flame out and be found in the darkness outside of the wedding feast.

1 John 2:8-11
8 Again, a new commandment I write unto you, which thing is true in him and in you: because the darkness is past, and the true light now shineth.
9 He that saith he is in the light, and hateth his brother, is in darkness even until now.
10 He that loveth his brother abideth in the light, and there is none occasion of stumbling in him.
11 But he that hateth his brother is in darkness, and walketh in darkness, and knoweth not whither he goeth, because that darkness hath blinded his eyes.

Love lights the way, but hatred blinds the eyes. True discipleship is shown in our love one for another.[192] Walking in love is well pleasing to our Lord and allows for the continual filling of the Holy Spirit's oil into our lamps.

Ephesians 5:8, 15-18
8 For ye were sometimes darkness, but now are ye light in the Lord: walk as children of light:
15 See then that ye walk circumspectly, not as fools, but as wise,
16 Redeeming the time, because the days are evil.
17 Wherefore be ye not unwise, but understanding what the will of the Lord is.
18 And be not drunk with wine, wherein is excess; but be filled with the Spirit;

---

[192] John 13:34-35.

CHAPTER 7

Dove

The gentle sacrifice that sanctifies

Without a doubt, the dove is the most recognized symbol for the Holy Spirit in Scripture and iconography. It did not become so through abundant use in the Bible—wind, water, and fire all appear with more frequency—but through a singularly prominent occurrence.

John 1:32-34
32 And John bare record, saying, I saw the Spirit descending from heaven like a dove, and it abode upon him.
33 And I knew him not: but he that sent me to baptize with water, the same said unto me, Upon whom thou shalt see the Spirit descending, and remaining on him, the same is he which baptizeth with the Holy Ghost.
34 And I saw, and bare record that this is the Son of God.

This event is recorded in all four Gospels and was seen both by John and Jesus.[193]

Mark 1:9-11
9 And it came to pass in those days, that Jesus came from Nazareth of Galilee, and was baptized of John in Jordan.
10 And straightway coming up out of the water, he saw the heavens opened, and the Spirit like a dove descending upon him:

---

[193] Matt. 3:16-17; Mark 1:9-11; Luke 3:21-22.

11 And there came a voice from heaven, saying, Thou art my beloved Son, in whom I am well pleased.

The Holy Spirit could have directed John to anoint Jesus with oil, but He didn't. He could have blown in as a giant windstorm on the river, but that didn't happen either. He could have shown up as a column of fire from heaven, but He reserved that for the day of Pentecost. On this most auspicious day—the inauguration of Jesus's public ministry—He appeared in the form of a dove. With all these other prominent and powerful symbols to choose from, why the dove?

Some iconography depicts the descending dove head down with its wings pointing backward. But doves do not land this way. They descend feet down, wings flapping. With wings outstretched and feet down, a dove descends in cruciform as it finds its footing. This is the exact message of the Holy Spirit as He came upon Jesus in the bodily form of the dove. Even as John proclaimed "Behold the Lamb of God!" to let the people on Jordan's banks know of God's perfect sacrifice, the Holy Spirit showed how it would be made and Who would lead Jesus there.

Hebrews 9:13-14
13 For if the blood of bulls and of goats, and the ashes of an heifer sprinkling the unclean, sanctifieth to the purifying of the flesh:
*14 How much more shall the blood of Christ, **who through the eternal Spirit offered himself without spot to God**, purge your conscience from dead works to serve the living God?* [Emphasis added.]

The predominant use of doves in Scripture is as sacrificial animals. When Jesus came out of Jordan's waters, the Holy Spirit appeared as a dove, giving prominence to the gentle and sacrificial nature of the Messiah. How doves live and the reasons and manner in which they were offered in the tabernacle and the temple provide us with many added insights into the Holy Spirit. Let us look at how they live first.

Dove Eyes

Doves and pigeons (same family, different size) are daytime birds—diurnal, not nocturnal. Being a creature of the day reminds us that we are to walk in the daylight of the Spirit.[194] Diurnal birds see better than any other daytime animal. "Very likely, the avian retina—with its high cone densities, deep foveae (depressions in the retina), near ultraviolet receptors, and colored oil droplets that interact with several core pigments—is the most capable diurnal retina of any animal."[195]

Doves can release colored oil droplets into their eyes that help filter out background colors. Yellow oil filters out a blue background and red oil filters out a green background. These oil filters—their anointed vision, if you will—enable them to discern objects with contrasting detail in a field of view that would otherwise overwhelm their vision. It is the Holy Spirit that graces us with the ability to discern spirits[196] and recognize truth.[197]

A dove sees better laterally than it does directly in front because its eyes are set on the sides of its head.[198] Have you have ever watched a dove's or a pigeon's head-bobbing walk? They do this to build depth perception one eye at a time.[199] In essence, they maintain singular vision, which for them is clearest up close. Dove vision is intimate.

Song of Solomon 4:1a, 9
1 Behold, thou art fair, my love; behold, thou art fair; thou hast doves'
eyes within thy locks...
9 Thou hast ravished my heart, my sister, my spouse; thou hast rav-
ished my heart with one of thine eyes, with one chain of thy neck.

---

[194] Eph. 5:8-9.
[195] Frank B. Gill, *Ornithology*, W. H. Freeman and Co., New York, 1990, p. 164.
[196] 1 Cor. 12:10.
[197] 1 John 2:27.
[198] Frank B. Gill, *Ornithology*, W. H. Freeman and Co., New York, 1990, p. 160.
[199] Miriam Sclein and Thomas Y. Cromwell, *Pigeons*, Junior Books, New York, 1989, p.14.

As the dove, the Holy Spirit intimately leads us in maintaining a singular vision so that we can be filled with light.

Matthew 6:22
The light of the body is the eye: if therefore thine eye be single, thy whole body shall be full of light.

Doves in Flight

Doves are swift, powerful fliers. Their feathers—smoother and stiffer than those of most other birds—even out the airflow around their bodies during flight. At the risk of mixing metaphors, not only is the Holy Spirit the wind that lifts us, He also provides us with the spiritual plumage to dramatically reduce drag as we abide under His wings.

Doves don't float, they flap. While eagles soar on thermals, wings outstretched, doves flap furiously through the air to fly. In doing so, their wings create noisy vortexes of air—especially on takeoff and landing. Some pigeons have special feathers that produce distinct sounds. They use these sounds to communicate with other pigeons while in flight. As we abide under the shadow of His wings, we need to be attentive to the truth He communicates to us.

Psalm 91:1, 4
1 He that dwelleth in the secret place of the most High shall abide under the shadow of the Almighty.
4 He shall cover thee with his feathers, and under his wings shalt thou trust: his truth shall be thy shield and buckler.

Doves have ten primary feathers on each wing. Ten is the number of the Law. When Moses met God on Mount Sinai, the Lord gave him two copies of the Ten Commandments written on tables of stone.[200] In the Jewish festival calendar, the Feast of Weeks—or Pentecost—

---

[200] Exod. 24:12; 31:18; 32:15-16.

commemorates the giving of the Law.[201] The promise of the New Covenant was to have the Law written in our hearts.[202] Jesus Christ, the living Torah, made this a reality when He wrote the law on our hearts with the Spirit of the living God.

2 Corinthians 3:3
Forasmuch as ye are manifestly declared to be the epistle of Christ ministered by us, written not with ink, but with the Spirit of the living God; not in tables of stone, but in fleshy tables of the heart.

Doves appear in ten references in the New Testament. Five of these references are to doves or pigeons as sacrificial animals (Matt. 21:12; Mark 11:15; Luke 2:24; John 2:14, 16) and bring to mind the requirements of the Law of Moses. The other five uses are in reference to the Holy Spirit either directly (Matt. 3:16; Mark 1:10; Luke 3:22; John 1:32) or in context (Matt. 10:16-20). The letter of the Law is insufficient to sustain us. We need the Spirit of the law—the law of the Spirit of life in Christ Jesus—to free us from the law of sin and death to serve the living God in peace.[203]

Rock doves produce seven times more heat in flight than at rest.[204] Like most birds, doves have no sweat glands with which to cool down. During flight, excess heat is dispersed by the passage of air through air sacks. When resting, doves cool down by panting. To avoid overheating, we need to let the wind of the Spirit go through us. We accomplish this by speaking out the truth He reveals within us.

Jeremiah 20:9
Then I said, "I will not make mention of Him, Nor speak anymore in His name." But His word was in my heart like a burning fire Shut up in my bones; I was weary of holding it back, And I could not. NKJV

---

[201] Jewish Virtual Library, "Jewish Holidays: Shavu'ot," http://www.jewishvirtuallibrary.org/shavu-ot (accessed September 11, 2017).

[202] Jer. 31:31-33.

[203] Rom. 2:28-29; 8:1-6.

[204] Frank B. Gill, *Ornithology*, W. H. Freeman and Co., New York, 1990, p. 114.

The lack of sweat glands speaks to us of resting in His grace and not striving in our own strength. Sweat is first mentioned in the Scripture as the result of the curse because of Adam's sin (Gen. 3:19). Before they sinned, Adam and Eve tended the garden and freely ate of all the trees God had planted for them, the only restriction being the tree of knowledge of good and evil. After the Fall, God told Adam that he would eat through sweaty toil. Jesus said that His yoke was easy and His burden was light (Matt. 11:30). Laboring for the Lord is supposed to be laboring *with* the Lord in the power of *His* strength. Ministering should not make us a sweaty mess.

Ezekiel 44:18
They [the priests] *shall have linen bonnets upon their heads, and shall have linen breeches upon their loins; they* [the priests] *shall not gird themselves with any thing that causeth sweat.*

The Lord did not want His servants sweating as they went about their daily ministrations in the temple. It is the Holy Spirit who empowers us to minister in His strength instead of striving in our flesh.

Colossians 1:29
Whereunto I also labour, striving according to his working, which worketh in me mightily.

Dove Diet
Doves and pigeons are the only type of birds that feed their squabs—their hatchlings—crop milk.[205] Called "pigeon's milk," doves start producing this secretion a couple of days before the eggs hatch. Pigeon's milk is a suspension of protein-rich and fat-rich cells that slough off from the lining of the crop. In addition to having a high protein and fat content, it also contains anti-oxidants and immune-enhancing factors like immunoglobulin A. Squabs cannot handle solid

---

[205] Ibid., p.539.

food when they hatch and must feed on milk for at least their first week outside the egg.[206]

1 Peter 2:2
As newborn babes, desire the sincere milk of the word, that ye may grow thereby:

Babes in Christ require milk, and the Holy Spirit is their nursemaid. As the dove, He gently feeds us with easily digestible, nutrient dense superfood designed to strengthen our developing, recreated spirit while protecting us from corrosion (spiritual anti-oxidants) and disease (spiritual antibodies). Following the Spirit's lead, when we disciple people to Christ we should do so using the milk of the Word—the first principles of the doctrine of Christ[207]—until they are mature enough to handle meat.

1 Corinthians 3:1-2
1 And I, brethren, could not speak unto you as unto spiritual, but as unto carnal, even as unto babes in Christ.
2 I have fed you with milk, and not with meat: for hitherto ye were not able to bear it, neither yet now are ye able.

Meat belongs to the mature. In the King James Bible, the word "meat" generally means solid food and can encompass vegetables and grains as well as flesh. The grain offering—"meat offering" in the KJV—in Leviticus 2:1 is made up of fine flour, olive oil, and frankincense. The oil and frankincense are garnishments to the main offering, which is ground grain. Grain is seed, and seeds are what mature doves feed on. Jesus uses seed as a symbol for the word of God.[208]

---

[206] Wikipedia, "Crop milk," https://en.wikipedia.org/wiki/Crop_milk (accessed September 13, 2017).
[207] These are repentance from dead works, faith toward God, the doctrine of baptisms, and the doctrines of the laying on of hands, the resurrection of the dead, and eternal judgment (Heb. 5:12-6:2).
[208] Luke 8:4-15.

As the dove, the Holy Spirit leads us in the digestion of the word of God so that we can assimilate its truth and grow thereby.

Most birds drink by dipping their beaks into the water and then tilting their heads back to let it run down their gullets. Doves are different. They stick their beaks into the water and suck it up as though through a straw. What is God telling us? Along with giving us spiritual milk and feeding us the word of God, the Holy Spirit empowers us to drink freely and fully from the river of life.

Revelation 22:17
And the Spirit and the bride say, Come. And let him that heareth say, Come. And let him that is athirst come. And whosoever will, let him take the water of life freely.

Doves in Love

In the Song of Solomon, the bridegroom calls his bride "my dove" and she says he has dove's eyes "by rivers of waters, washed with milk."[209] Israel is also referred to as a dove in Scripture.[210] The mating habits of doves illustrate God's way of wooing us to His loving embrace. The male dove courts the female with an avian dance, demonstrating the Holy Spirit's work in bringing the sinner to Christ.

During courtship, the male bows and coos to the female, while the female watches. The male is the one who initiates the relationship. Likewise, it is the Holy Spirit that pursues us. We love Him because He first loved us. His first step in the dance is the conviction of sin because we have not believed in Jesus.[211] As we read above in Revelation 22:17, the Spirit calls the thirsty to drink the water of life.

After the male bows and coos, the two birds then begin to smooth each other's feathers. This speaks to us of comfort and worship. God brings

---

[209] Song of Sol. 2:14; 5:12.
[210] Isa. 60:8.
[211] John 16:8-9.

comforting peace to our souls, and we worship Him in response. At this point in the dance, the male dove feeds the female a few seeds. We have seen that the word of God is spoken of as seed. Ground seed is baked into bread, which Jesus broke for His disciples during the Last Supper. When we are born again by faith in Jesus Christ, the Spirit takes up habitation in our hearts. Peter calls this being born again of incorruptible seed.

1 Peter 1:23
Being born again, not of corruptible seed, but of incorruptible, by the word of God, which liveth and abideth for ever.

The dove's courtship continues for several days and culminates in their mating. Pigeons and doves mate for life. The Comforter abides with us forever.[212]

After mating, the male dove builds a nest. Jesus said He would build His church.[213] The female only lays one or two eggs per clutch. When applying this to our Spirit-led evangelism, I see it as an illustration of our reaching out to the individual versus the crowd. Though our voices can reach many—particularly in this digital age—our hearts can only focus on a few. God gives doves small families to raise. This speaks of focus and intimacy, the Holy Spirit concentrating on the one coming to Christ. Both parents sit on the eggs, and both feed the young. Evangelism and discipleship are joint efforts between the Holy Spirit and us.[214]

These are some of the lessons we learn from how doves live. Let us turn now to how they were offered.

---

[212] John 14:16-17.
[213] Matt. 16:18, "rock" in this verse is not a reference to Peter, but to Christ Himself. Peter is *petros* in the Greek, a piece of rock. Rock is *petra* in the Greek, a massive rock.
[214] Rev. 22:17; 1 Cor. 3:9.

The Clean and the Unclean

The Lord classified animals as clean or unclean early in the Biblical record.[215] The major distinction between the two was that clean animals were sacrificed to the Lord, whereas the unclean were not. Later, clean animals became part of the authorized diet of the covenant community.[216] Whereas the types of clean mammals, fish, and insects are delineated, unclean birds are specifically identified. Scripture does not provide a list or description of clean birds, only the unclean. The people of God were to walk circumspectly, differentiating between the clean and the unclean.

Leviticus 20:24-26

24 But I have said unto you, Ye shall inherit their land, and I will give it unto you to possess it, a land that floweth with milk and honey: I am the Lord your God, which have separated you from other people.

25 Ye shall therefore put difference between clean beasts and unclean, and between unclean fowls and clean: and ye shall not make your souls abominable by beast, or by fowl, or by any manner of living thing that creepeth on the ground, which I have separated from you as unclean.

26 And ye shall be holy unto me: for I the Lord am holy, and have severed you from other people, that ye should be mine.

Not only was it forbidden to eat unclean birds, but they also became emblematic of evil spirits.

Revelation 18:2

And he cried mightily with a loud voice, saying, "Babylon the great is fallen, is fallen, and has become a dwelling place of demons, a prison for every foul spirit, and a cage for every unclean and hated bird! NKJV

---

[215] Gen. 7:1-3; 8:20.
[216] Lev. 11; Deut. 14:3-8.

Ravens are classified as unclean birds. Doves are clean birds as evidenced by their use as sacrificial animals. This is intriguing as we review the story of Noah.

Lessons from the Ark

Genesis 8:6-9

6 So it came to pass, at the end of forty days, that Noah opened the window of the ark which he had made.

7 Then he sent out a raven, which kept going to and fro until the waters had dried up from the earth.

8 He also sent out from himself a dove, to see if the waters had receded from the face of the ground.

9 But the dove found no resting place for the sole of her foot, and she returned into the ark to him, for the waters were on the face of the whole earth. So he put out his hand and took her, and drew her into the ark to himself. NKJV

At the end of the cataclysmic event, Noah sent out a carrion bird and a seed eater to spy for land. The raven decided to remain on the wing going "to and fro" until land appeared.[217] It did not return to the ark, presumably because there were enough dead bodies floating about to satisfy its hunger. Like evil spirits, ravens feed on rottenness. Evil spirits find perch on the ground of death-dealing, corrosive sin. Doves are too gentle for that. They would rather come home to roost than ride on dead bodies in the waves of doubt and decay.

In this account, Noah stands as a type of the Father. Evil spirits do the Lord's bidding[218] but do not abide with Him.[219] Though Noah sent out both birds, he sent the dove out "from himself" (v. 8). Both birds were sent out at the same time. Scripture tells us that we are to test the spirits to see if they are from God (1 John 4:1-3). While the raven wandered, the dove returned to the ark and Noah drew her "to himself."

---

[217] This is reminiscent of Satan's description of his own travels in Job 2:2.

[218] 1 Sam. 16:14; 1 Kings 22:19-23.

[219] Ezek. 28:16; John 14:30.

The dove's interaction with Noah gives us a glimpse of the relationship between God the Father and God the Holy Spirit. In the words of the Nicene Creed:

> "And I believe in the Holy Ghost,
> The Lord and giver of life,
> Who proceedeth from the Father;
> Who with the Father and the Son together is worshipped and glorified."[220]

Genesis 8:10-12
10 And he waited yet another seven days, and again he sent the dove out from the ark.
11 Then the dove came to him in the evening, and behold, a freshly plucked olive leaf was in her mouth; and Noah knew that the waters had receded from the earth.
12 So he waited yet another seven days and sent out the dove, which did not return again to him anymore. NKJV

Noah sent the dove out in seven-day intervals. This speaks to us of seasons of outpouring and visitation in the Father's timetable. His way is not our way. It is not incumbent upon Him to conform to our pressures and timetables. It is the responsibility (read "response-ability") of the saint to be aware of the moves of God. Birds know their seasons. God expects no less from us.

Jeremiah 8:7
Even the stork in the sky knows her appointed seasons, and the dove, the swift and the thrush observe the time of their migration. But my people do not know the requirements of the Lord. NIV

---

[220] This is the Orthodox version of the Creed which is nearest to the one originally crafted in the fourth century. Orthodox Church in America, "The Creed: The Symbol of Faith," https://oca.org/orthodoxy/prayers/symbol-of-faith (accessed September 24, 2017).

When we are led of the Spirit, we are sensitive to the movements of the Dove. We will know the times of our migration, the requirements of the Lord, and the signs of the times. Since the Spirit comes from the Father, He is able to reveal to us the Father's desires, plans, and intentions. Our level of responsiveness to His revelation determines our readiness and the frequency we are found to be in the right place at the right time.

Genesis 8:11 tells us that the dove returned the second time with an olive leaf "in her mouth." Dove in this passage is a feminine noun in the Hebrew and, as such, "her" is properly translated. Dove in the Greek is also a feminine noun. This is a concept that may be unfamiliar to readers who only speak English. Our nouns are not gendered, although students of Romance languages such as Spanish or French may have learned about them. That the word "dove" happens to be a female-gendered noun in both languages may seem on the surface to be inconsequential. After all, linguists will tell you there is nothing particularly feminine or masculine about the object the word represents. The gender is just its grammatical form.

That being said, it behooves us to remember that God invented language, and the Holy Spirit inspired the writing of Scripture in the languages within which it was encoded. Though God is portrayed primarily in the masculine (e.g., He, Father, Son), there are motherly metaphors made in Scripture regarding the Godhead. Jesus's proclamation over Jerusalem is perhaps the one most familiar of all:

Matthew 23:37
O Jerusalem, Jerusalem, thou that killest the prophets, and stonest them which are sent unto thee, how often would I have gathered thy children together, even as a hen gathereth her chickens under her wings, and ye would not!

Based on bird behavior, all the mentions of abiding under His wings carry with them this nuance. If you have never seen a lonely puffed-up hen waddling through the yard, only to discover that she was hiding her chicks from view, you have missed a precious sight indeed. These maternal protective instincts also find expression in the proverbial mama-bear syndrome.

Hosea 13:8
I will meet them as a bear that is bereaved of her whelps, and will rend the caul of their heart, and there will I devour them like a lion: the wild beast shall tear them.

Traditional culture defaults to seeing mother as the comforter and father as the protector. As we see in the verse above, mothers are far from averse to action when protecting their young, and as we see below, fathers bring comfort as well.

Isaiah 66:13
As one whom his mother comforteth, so will I comfort you; and ye shall be comforted in Jerusalem.

Even though the preponderance of Scripture refers to God in the masculine, we do well to remember that when God created man in His own image, He created them male and female.[221] This tells us that the woman is as much an image bearer of God as is the man. If maleness is our only view of the Godhead, we are not seeing the complete picture. Of the three Persons, the Father and Son are most directly identified as male. In contrast, two of the symbols used for the Holy Spirit—the dove and the eagle—carry with them the mark of femininity.

Deuteronomy 32:11-12
11 As an eagle stirreth up her nest, fluttereth over her young, spreadeth abroad her wings, taketh them, beareth them on her wings:

---

[221] Gen. 1:27.

12 So the Lord alone did lead him, and there was no strange god with him.

As we will see in more detail in Chapter 8, the Hebrew term translated "fluttereth" in verse 11 is the same word translated as "moved" in the King James Version of Genesis 1:2 with regard to the Spirit's interaction with the face of the waters.

The dove came back to Noah bearing an olive leaf. This scene is the source of the classic symbol for peace, the dove with the olive branch. When we apply what we learned in the examination of the anointing oil, we can see that it is the Holy Spirit who brings the anointing to us.

The Offering
Once Noah unloaded the ark, he took the time to thank God for bringing them through.

Genesis 8:20
*And Noah builded an altar unto the Lord; and took of every clean beast, and of **every clean fowl**, and offered burnt offerings on the altar.* [Emphasis added.]

From the subsequent testimony of Scripture, we know that Noah sacrificed some doves and pigeons on that day. There are peculiarities in how birds were sacrificed and offered that we need to examine next.

Genesis 15:8-10
8 And he said, "Lord God, how shall I know that I will inherit it?"
9 So He said to him, "Bring Me a three-year-old heifer, a three-year-old female goat, a three-year-old ram, a turtledove, and a young pigeon."
*10 Then he brought all these to Him and cut them in two, down the middle, and placed each piece opposite the other; **but he did not cut the birds in two.** NKJV* [Emphasis added.]

The animals were divided symmetrically and represented the two parties entering into the agreement. The slaughtered animals testified of the penalty for breaking the covenant.[222] Note, however, that instead of taking one bird and dividing it, Abraham took two equivalent birds and laid them side by side. This method of sacrifice was later codified in the law of Moses.

Leviticus 1:14-17
14 And if the burnt sacrifice for his offering to the Lord be of fowls, then he shall bring his offering of turtledoves, or of young pigeons.
15 And the priest shall bring it unto the altar, and wring off his head, and burn it on the altar; and the blood thereof shall be wrung out at the side of the altar:
16 And he shall pluck away his crop with his feathers, and cast it beside the altar on the east part, by the place of the ashes:
17 And he shall cleave it with the wings thereof, but shall not divide it asunder: and the priest shall burn it upon the altar, upon the wood that is upon the fire: it is a burnt sacrifice, an offering made by fire, of a sweet savour unto the Lord.

"Wring off his head" in verse fifteen sounds like a decapitation, but it is not. The Hebrew word is *malaq* and means "to wring the neck of a fowl without separating it." This can be clearly seen in the direction given in Leviticus 5:8.

Leviticus 5:8
*He is to bring them to the cohen, who will offer the one for a sin offering first. He is to **wring its neck but not remove the head***, CJB [Emphasis added.]

In summary, following are the steps the priest took in sacrificing doves and pigeons:

- The neck was snapped and the throat torn open without removing the head.
- The blood was squeezed out of the body.
- The bird was torn open, spreading its rib cage.
- Feathers and innards were removed.
- The body of the bird was placed on the wood of the altar as a burnt sacrifice.

If the reader has never hunted doves, all this sounds rather gruesome. What could it possibly tell us about the Holy Spirit?

The Unity of the Spirit
We begin with the fact that the bird was not bisected or beheaded. This speaks to us of the unity of the Spirit. As Ephesians 4:3-4 informs us, we are to keep the unity of the Spirit, for there is One Spirit. It is important to remember this when considering the gifts of the Spirit. After listing the nine facets of the manifestation of the Spirit, the apostle Paul states:

1 Corinthians 12:11
But one and the same Spirit works all these things, distributing to each one individually as He wills. NKJV

Two different saints may speak in two different supernaturally endowed languages, but they are both distributed and energized by the same Holy Spirit. The saint is not given a separate "tongue spirit" or "healing spirit" or "spirit of discernment." Rather, the Holy Spirit exhibits His character and power *through* the saint in tongues, healing, or discerning of spirits as well as the other manifestation and ministry gifts. Because our God is relational and desires to work with and through us, the way the Holy Spirit expresses Himself through the saint is unique to that particular saint's identity. Permit me an analogy.

A master composer has a grand symphony. Inside this piece of music, there are times when all of the instruments are playing the same melody, and other times when they are playing different refrains that are picked up by other sections later in the composition. Violins and flutes may play the same melody at the same time—it is the same musical message—but the sound and impact they make will be distinctly their own. Flutes sound like flutes, not violins. But even in the instrument group itself, the individual instruments have their own unique tones because of the uniqueness of their manufacture (e.g., age, wood or metal type, etc.) and the person who is playing them. The same composer leads them to play the same music, but the master's music is being expressed through uniquely equipped musicians.

Manifestation gifts are like the melody that everybody plays. But how the music comes through is unique to the saint who brings it forth. Ministry gifts are like the refrains written for particular sections. Yet once again, how they are practiced is uniquely fitted to the servant who performs them. When the saintly orchestra keeps the unity of Spirit, our parts are played at the right time in the right way and make a joyful noise that proclaims the goodness and greatness of God.

The Significance of the Head
The dove's neck was broken, but its head was not removed. This is an odd inefficiency. The priest would have to take care not to be too forceful, and the dangling head could impede the flow of the blood from the bird's body. It would be much simpler to wring the head completely off and toss it out of the way. But the Holy Spirit had a deeper purpose than mere efficiency in the prescribed manner of sacrifice.

Before the cross, it was the Holy Spirit that led Jesus. The Spirit brought Him to Mary's womb (Luke 1:35). The Spirit led Him into the wilderness to be tempted by the devil (Matt. 4:1). The Spirit sent Him to heal the broken-hearted (Luke 4:18). The Spirit led Him to and through the cross (Mark 14:38; Heb. 9:14).

After the Ascension, it is Jesus who directs the Holy Spirit. He sent the Comforter down to convict the world of sin, righteousness, and judgment (John 16:7-11). He poured the Spirit out on the apostles on the day of Pentecost (Acts 2:33). When Jesus was on the earth, it was the Spirit who anointed His preaching (Luke 4:18). Now that Jesus sits on the right hand of the Father, it is the Spirit who speaks for Jesus (John 16:13-15). Once Jesus was glorified, the Spirit submitted Himself to the headship of the Son (John 7:37-39). This is the message of the intact but disabled head of the dove. All that the Spirit directs us to do He does so under the leadership of Jesus who is the head over everything for the church (Eph. 1:22).

The Shadow of His Wings
Sacrifices were instituted to make atonement for sins. The Hebrew word translated as "atonement" is *kaphar*, which means "to coat or cover over." Cracking the dove's ribcage open expands the area covered under the shadow of his wings and exposes his heart. In the same way, after Jesus offered Himself on the cross, the Spirit could be poured out to cover us and allow us entry into the heart of God.

1 Corinthians 2:9-10
9 But as it is written, Eye hath not seen, nor ear heard, neither have entered into the heart of man, the things which God hath prepared for them that love him.
10 But God hath revealed them unto us by his Spirit: for the Spirit searcheth all things, yea, the deep things of God.

Placed on the Wood of the Altar
As stated at the beginning of this chapter, the Dove's descent on Jesus in Jordan's waters foretold of His crucifixion. Every bird sacrificed and laid on the altar prefigured our Lord led of the Spirit to be nailed to the tree. In the language of the burnt offering, His was a sweet smelling sacrifice unto God.[223] His offering was the ultimate expres-

---

[223] Lev. 1:17; Eph. 5:2.

153

sion of love.[224] It is the Holy Spirit who brings this love to us and through us.

2 Timothy 1:7
For God hath not given us the spirit of fear; but of power, and of love, and of a sound mind.

From Conviction to Confession to Communion

These sacrificial realities, particularly the technical applications of the sin and burnt offerings, show us the Holy Spirit's leading into full communion with God.[225] The sin or guilt offering was presented when someone became aware of their sin. This indicates that when the sin was originally committed, the person was unaware of having caused an offence. But once aware, they had to bring a sin offering for atonement.

Leviticus 5:1-4 lists several instances in which a person might sin and not know it. But the law makes it clear that as soon as one realizes it, he or she bears guilt in the matter and is required to make atonement.

Leviticus 5:5-7
5 'And it shall be, when he is guilty in any of these matters, that he shall confess that he has sinned in that thing;
6 and he shall bring his trespass offering to the Lord for his sin which he has committed, a female from the flock, a lamb or a kid of the goats as a sin offering. So the priest shall make atonement for him concerning his sin.
7 'If he is not able to bring a lamb, then he shall bring to the Lord, for his trespass which he has committed, two turtledoves or two young pigeons: one as a sin offering and the other as a burnt offering. NKJV

---

[224] John 15:13; Gal. 2:20.
[225] For a fuller treatment of this, please refer to "A Blood-Cleared Conscience," which is Chapter 6 of my book *The Blood of Jesus Christ*.

The Holy Spirit convicts us of sin to lead us to confession. This role is illustrated in the first dove sacrificed as a sin offering in that: "He shall confess that he has sinned in that thing." The Comforter has come to be Jesus's advocate within us. He lovingly reveals to us aspects of our actions that we were unaware were sinful and offensive to our Lord. Our first response to this conviction should be confession.

1 John 1:8-10
8 If we say that we have no sin, we deceive ourselves, and the truth is not in us.
9 If we confess our sins, he is faithful and just to forgive us our sins, and to cleanse us from all unrighteousness.
10 If we say that we have not sinned, we make him a liar, and his word is not in us.

The second dove was offered as a burnt offering. This free-will offering expressed thankfulness and worship to the Lord because of His forgiveness. It is this stage of being set free from sin that is neglected far too frequently. Most of us have been taught that we need to confess our sins, and are very intent on doing just that.

But often, we do not move on from acknowledging forgiveness granted and thanking God for it. We keep coming back to the foot of the cross, confessing the same breach over and over. The Spirit would have us move through the cross and acknowledge forgiveness over the sin through our worship, giving thanks to the One who set us free.

This is the significance of the dove as a burnt offering, for the Spirit not only convicts us of sin, righteousness, and judgment; He also leads us in worship.

John 4:24
God is a Spirit: and they that worship him must worship him in spirit and in truth.

Doves at Rest

Psalm 55:6

And I said, Oh that I had wings like a dove! for then would I fly away, and be at rest.

The Holy Spirit enables us to escape from trouble and find rest. The Hebrew word translated "rest" is *shakan* and means "to settle down, abide, dwell, to tabernacle, to reside." The Spirit not only brings the cause of Christ to our conscience, but He also encourages us in our times of trouble and trial,[226] exhorting us to press forward to attain the prize of our high calling of God in Christ Jesus.[227] He leads us in being participants in this effort with one another through the distribution of tongues, interpretation of tongues, and prophecy.[228]

As Christ's representative on earth, it is the Holy Spirit who brings to us the reality of the rest that Jesus promises to all who come to Him.

Matthew 11:28-30

28 Come unto me, all ye that labour and are heavy laden, and I will give you rest.

29 Take my yoke upon you, and learn of me; for I am meek and lowly in heart: and ye shall find rest unto your souls.

30 For my yoke is easy, and my burden is light.

The principle of rest speaks to us of abiding in His presence. The Psalmist speaks of this as being under the shadow of His wings.[229]

Psalm 61:4

I will abide in thy tabernacle for ever: I will trust in the covert of thy wings. Selah.

---

[226] 2 Cor. 1:4; 1 Cor. 10:13.

[227] Phil. 3:13-15.

[228] 1 Cor. 14:1-31.

[229] See also Ps. 17:8; 36:7; 57:1; 63:7; and 91:1.

From the gentle dove, we move on to the lion of the skies, the eagle. As the dove leads us to rest, the eagle leads us to war. Though these two symbols share common ground in that they are both birds, the differences between doves and eagles give us a glimpse of the breadth of the Holy Spirit's personality. As Jesus is the Lamb and the Lion, the Holy Spirit is the dove and the eagle. Let us soar on to the next chapter.

CHAPTER 8

Eagle

Executing judgment on wings of eagles

The eagle appears early in Scripture as a symbol for the Holy Spirit.

Genesis 1:1-2
1 In the beginning God created the Heaven and the earth.
2 And the earth was without form, and void; and darkness was upon the face of the deep. And the Spirit of God moved upon the face of the waters.

The Hebrew word translated "moved" in verse 2 is *rachaph*. The image of how the Spirit of God moved upon the face of the primordial waters is given to us in Deuteronomy, where *rachaph* is translated "fluttereth."

Deuteronomy 32:11-12
11 As an eagle stirreth up her nest, fluttereth over her young, spreadeth abroad her wings, taketh them, beareth them on her wings:
12 So the Lord alone did lead him, and there was no strange god with him.

The Spirit of God fluttered over the waters like an eagle over her young. And like an eagle, the Spirit led Israel out of Egypt.

Isaiah 63:11-14

11 Then he remembered the days of old, of Moses and his people. Where is he who brought them up out of the sea with the shepherds of his flock? Where is he who put in the midst of them his Holy Spirit,

12 who caused his glorious arm to go at the right hand of Moses, who divided the waters before them to make for himself an everlasting name,

13 who led them through the depths? Like a horse in the desert, they did not stumble.

14 Like livestock that go down into the valley, the Spirit of the Lord gave them rest. So you led your people, to make for yourself a glorious name. ESV

God put His Spirit in the midst of His people and led them to liberty and rest. Moses described this as an eagle stirring up her nest with fluttering wings that ultimately stretch out and bear her young on the wind until they are ready to fly. Moses came by this analogy from the mouth of the Lord Himself.

Exodus 19:4
*Ye have seen what I did unto the Egyptians, and **how I bare you on eagles' wings**, and brought you unto myself.* [Emphasis added.]

Even as Isaiah's description highlights three typical functions of the Holy Spirit—leading, power (spoken of as His "glorious arm"), and granting rest—so Moses gives us three earmarks of life with the Spirit.

Deuteronomy 32:13
He made him ride on the heights of the land and fed him with the fruit of the fields. He nourished him with honey from the rock, and with oil from the flinty crag, NIV

"Fruit of the fields" speaks to us of the fruit of the Spirit.[230] Honey is a symbol for the sweetness of the word of God received in revelation,[231] and oil speaks to us of the anointing. This is a description of what it is like to walk in the Spirit and is given as the result of the Lord stirring up His people as an eagle stirs her nest. On the wind of those wings, let us fly into the nature of eagles to find what God would teach us about His Spirit.

The Golden Eagle

All eagles are eagles and, as such, share many commonalities. This may sound overly obvious, but I mention it for a reason. Most of the Christian decorations with an eagle motif marketed in the United States feature the bald eagle. While this is savvy marketing—the bald eagle is our national bird, after all—it is bad iconography. The bald eagle is a sea eagle native to North America. The holy men of God who were inspired to write Scripture did not have this eagle in mind when they employed eagle analogies.

The eagle behavior described in Deuteronomy 32 is that of the female golden eagle. Golden eagles are the most populous type of eagle in the world, and it is this type of eagle that Scripture mentions most frequently. The golden eagle is also known as the true booted eagle, because it has feathers that go all the way down to its feet.

On Wings of Eagles

The golden eagle takes off with powerful flaps of his wings. How powerful? Powerful enough to pluck a mountain goat off a cliff and fly it out over the gorge to drop it down to its death for later feasting. By contrast, bald eagles catch notably smaller prey—fish. It is helpful the have the right bird in mind when reading the Bible. With wingspans ranging from six to over seven feet wide, golden eagles are most spectacular when soaring. Wings outstretched, they ride on thermals—

---

[230] Gal. 5:22-23.
[231] See Ezek. 3:1-4 and Rev. 10:9-11.

updrafts of air created by solar heat—that carry them up into the atmosphere to heights sometimes approaching 14,000 feet.[232]

In choosing to use the eagle as a symbol of Himself, the Holy Spirit also incorporated the wind by nature of how eagles fly. Along with thermals, eagles also ride on the updrafts created when winds strike a cliff or mountain face and are forced to climb. Eagles can soar on these winds for hours on end at speeds as high as 44 miles per hour[233] with little effort. This is a picture of working in His strength. As the eagle, He gives us strength to bear burdens. As the wind, He causes us to soar on the heights without exhaustion.

Deuteronomy 28:49
The Lord shall bring a nation against thee from far, from the end of the earth, as swift as the eagle flieth; a nation whose tongue thou shalt not understand;

Scripture describes eagles as swift fliers[234] for good reason. When diving for prey—a picture the Lord uses of impending judgment—eagles can reach speeds of up to 200 miles per hour. As the dove's offering and its mournful coo speak to us of the Holy Spirit's work in the conviction of sin,[235] so the screech and dive of the eagle speak to us of His judgment.

Revelation 8:13
Then I looked, and I heard an eagle crying with a loud voice as it flew directly overhead, "Woe, woe, woe to those who dwell on the earth, at

---

[232] Helen Roney Sattler, *The Book of Eagles*, Lothrop, Lee & Shepard Books, New York, 1989, p. 12.

[233] Joe Van Wormer, *Eagles*, Lodestar Books, E. P. Dutton, New York, 1985, p. 5.

[234] The Hebrew word used is *da'ah*, to fly fast or swiftly. It is only used in four places: Deut. 28:49; Ps. 18:10; Jer. 48:40; and Jer. 49:22. All of these uses are in the context of judgment.

[235] Sin offering: Lev. 5:1-7. Dove moaning: Isa. 38:14, 17; Isa. 59:11-12; and Ezek. 7:16.

the blasts of the other trumpets that the three angels are about to blow!" ESV

All birds molt, but eagles do not lose all their large wing feathers in a single annual molt. They retain their flying ability while old feathers fall off and new ones take their place.[236] This is what David was singing about when He praised God for renewing our strength like the eagle's.[237] Isaiah takes up the same refrain in his encouragement to the saints.

Isaiah 40:29-31
29 He giveth power to the faint; and to them that have no might he increaseth strength.
30 Even the youths shall faint and be weary, and the young men shall utterly fall:
31 But they that wait upon the Lord shall renew their strength; they shall mount up with wings as eagles; they shall run, and not be weary; and they shall walk, and not faint.

Fasting and Feasting
Eagles learn to fly through fasting. Eaglets are voracious eaters, consuming as much as an adult bird. But once the eaglets are old enough to try their wings, the mother eagle begins to cut their ration and encourage hunger. This hunger in turn works on their instinctual wiring, driving their desire to hunt.[238] The mother will perch on a branch away from the nest holding meat in her talons. She calls her young to this dinner table in high-pitched squeaks. The eaglets stretch out their wings, hop tentatively out of the nest, and take their first flights toward the food offered by their mother.[239]

---

[236] Wormer, p. 9.
[237] Ps. 103:5. See also Eph. 3:16.
[238] Wormer, p. 34.
[239] Merebeth Switzer, *Nature's Children: Eagles*, Grolier Limited, Canada, 1985, p. 6.

Matthew 6:17-18

17 But you, when you fast, anoint your head and wash your face,

18 so that you do not appear to men to be fasting, but to your Father who is in the secret place; and your Father who sees in secret will reward you openly. NKJV

Jesus is the master of deeply layered meaning. We need to pay careful attention to His instruction and admonition. First, note that He says, "When you fast" not "If you fast." Seasons of abstaining from food to fuel more fervent prayer and devotion is a required practice of Christian discipleship. Secondly, the Lord instructs us to anoint our heads and wash our faces when we fast. This direction is given in contrast to the behavior of hypocrites who conceal their religious pride with a crusty countenance and disheveled hair.

In addition to the practical, physical application of this behavior to assure genuine fasting for the Father's approval only, I believe He has also given us great spiritual instruction. We should anoint our heads (be mindful and attentive to the Holy Spirit's oiling of our prayers) and wash our faces (bathe our countenance and outlook in His wellspring of life and God's life-giving Word) when we fast. In such a manner, we are made ready for the meat our Father would feed us.

Acts 13:1-3

1 Now there were in the church that was at Antioch certain prophets and teachers; as Barnabas, and Simeon that was called Niger, and Lucius of Cyrene, and Manaen, which had been brought up with Herod the tetrarch, and Saul.

2 As they ministered to the Lord, and fasted, the Holy Ghost said, Separate me Barnabas and Saul for the work whereunto I have called them.

3 And when they had fasted and prayed, and laid their hands on them, they sent them away.

Paul the apostle spent many years as Saul, a preaching disciple of Christ. When Antioch opened up to the gospel, he was installed as a teacher in that church.[240] While fasting in ministry to Jesus, the Holy Spirit set him free to fly to new territories to proclaim the gospel. This event was the commencement of Saul's and Barnabas's apostolic ministry.[241]

The dietary differences between squabs and eaglets speak to us of the range and direction of the Holy Spirit's leading through the words of life. Recall that doves feed their squabs pigeon's milk. This is the Spirit gently nurturing of us with the milk of the Word. Eaglets are fed raw meat and blood.

Job 39:27-30
27 Doth the eagle mount up at thy command, and make her nest on high?
28 She dwelleth and abideth on the rock, upon the crag of the rock, and the strong place.
29 From thence she seeketh the prey, and her eyes behold afar off.
30 Her young ones also suck up blood: and where the slain are, there is she.

Meat belongs to the mature. Jesus said that those who ate his flesh and drank his blood dwelt in Him and had eternal life.[242] This is the eagle diet that the Holy Spirit serves us. "Where the slain are, there is she," the Lord told Job. Jesus picked up this refrain while instructing his disciples about the battles to come.[243] Eagles are war birds taking prey out of the air, land, and sea, showing us the battlefields that the Holy Spirit leads us into.

---

[240] Barnabas was a prophet. See Acts 4:36. His name was Joseph. The apostles called him "bar nabas," son of prophecy.
[241] See Acts 14:14 and Gal. 2:7-9.
[242] John 6:53-58.
[243] Matt. 24:27-30.

164

God's original grant and commandment to man was for them to have dominion over the creatures of the sea, air, and earth.[244] He later forbid them from making idols out of anything in the heavens, the earth, or the waters.[245] Scripture teaches us that idols are nothing more than representations of demons.[246] These wicked beings advance the devil's twisted agenda in the very realms granted by God for man's dominion. The Holy Spirit leads us into battle to confront these influences and impose the rightful kingdom of Christ upon them.

Revelation 12:11-12
11 And they overcame him by the blood of the Lamb, and by the word of their testimony; and they loved not their lives unto the death.
12 Therefore rejoice, ye heavens, and ye that dwell in them. Woe to the inhabiters of the earth and of the sea! for the devil is come down unto you, having great wrath, because he knoweth that he hath but a short time.

Eaglets grow quickly on their diet of meat. An eaglet can weight up to forty times what it did at hatching within forty-five days. If humans did that, seven-week-old infants would weigh up to 300 pounds.[247] While this would clearly be unhealthy for a physical baby—not to mention the poor parents that had to carry it around—it is highly beneficial for spiritual babies. Eagles only feed their babies the good stuff. They tear the meat off their prey and feed it to their young. The adults are not as neat with their own plates.

An adult eagle eats every part of its prey—feathers, fur, scales, bones, and all. Its stomach can sort out the good food from the pieces that are of no value. The parts that cannot be digested are coughed up in the form of hard pellets.[248] Strong meat belongs to the mature, those who

---

[244] Gen. 1:26-28.
[245] Deut. 5:8.
[246] Lev. 17:7; Deut. 32:16-17; 1 Cor. 10:19-20.
[247] Sattler, p. 41.
[248] Switzer, p. 29.

have exercised their senses to distinguish between good and evil. As ambassadors of Christ, we feed new Christians solid meat from the Word of God. Their spiritual stomachs grow up knowing good food. When they are mature and led out by the Holy Spirit to various hunting grounds—different churches, ministries, books, and teaching—they are able to eat the meat and spit out the bones. This developmental picture of the eagle's diet is a great object lesson for how the Spirit of truth (John 15:26) teaches us the truth (1 John 2:20, 27) and helps us discern truth from error (1 John 4:6).

Deuteronomy 32 says the Lord led His people "as an eagle stirs up its nest."[249] The Hebrew word translated "stirs up" is *'ur'* and means to rouse one from sleep and cause him to open his eyes.

Isaiah 50:4-5
4 The Lord God has given me the tongue of those who are taught, that I may know how to sustain with a word him who is weary. Morning by morning he awakens; he awakens my ear to hear as those who are taught.
5 The Lord God has opened my ear, and I was not rebellious; I turned not backward. ESV

Once again, we have a beautiful picture of the Holy Spirit instructing us in His truth. He wakes us to His truth and teaches us to the point that we can teach and sustain others while keeping us moving forward with Him. The eagle wakens her young with the intent of seeing them fly, of seeing them fulfill the ultimate destiny of their hatching. The Holy Spirit wakens us to fulfill our destiny in Christ and reach out to the world around us with Christ's light of love.[250]

Open ears lead to open eyes, which bring us to the eagle's legendary vision.

---

[249] Deut. 32:11.
[250] See Eph. 5:13-16 and Rom. 13:9-14.

Eagle Eyes

Unlike doves, which are born blind, eagles hatch with their eyes wide open.[251]

Acts 26:15-18

15 And I said, Who art thou, Lord? And he said, I am Jesus whom thou persecutest.

16 But rise, and stand upon thy feet: for I have appeared unto thee for this purpose, to make thee a minister and a witness both of these things which thou hast seen, and of those things in the which I will appear unto thee;

17 Delivering thee from the people, and from the Gentiles, unto whom now I send thee,

18 To open their eyes, and to turn them from darkness to light, and from the power of Satan unto God, that they may receive forgiveness of sins, and inheritance among them which are sanctified by faith that is in me.

Saul was physically blinded during his encounter with Jesus on the road to Damascus. But his spiritual eyes were wide open,[252] and he received a commission from the Lord to open the eyes of others. The Holy Spirit can cause us to see truth previously incomprehensible to us. Saul, a man who had dedicated himself to the study of the Torah under one of the most prominent teachers of his day, failed to see the Savior the Law testified about. But when he met Jesus, the Anointed One who anoints us with the Holy Spirit, his eyes were opened to the truths he had studied for a lifetime. This is how he was able to enter the synagogues and preach Christ unto them so soon after his conversion.

---

[251] The Robinson Research World of Knowledge, www.robinsonresearch.com/ANIMALS/BIRDS/eagles.htm p. 4 (accessed March 12, 2001).

[252] Acts 9:11-12.

Acts 9:17-20

17 And Ananias went his way, and entered into the house; and putting his hands on him said, Brother Saul, the Lord, even Jesus, that appeared unto thee in the way as thou camest, hath sent me, that thou mightest receive thy sight, and be filled with the Holy Ghost.

18 And immediately there fell from his eyes as it had been scales: and he received sight forthwith, and arose, and was baptized.

19 And when he had received meat, he was strengthened. Then was Saul certain days with the disciples which were at Damascus.

20 And straightway he preached Christ in the synagogues, that he is the Son of God.

An eagle's eyes can be as large as a man's.[253] Its brain, however, is much smaller than ours. A golden eagle's brain weighs slightly less than half an ounce,[254] while the average human brain weighs about 3 pounds. More than 50% of our brain's surface area is devoted to processing visual information.[255] Considering that an eagle receives as much visual input—if not more—than a person does, it is not an understatement to say that vision dominates an eagle's thought life. If we had eyes that were proportioned to our brains in the same ratio as an eagle's, they would be the size of baseballs. Knowing that, it is not hard to understand how it is that an eagle's eyes have eight times the resolution power (focusing ability) of human eyes.[256]

In the Old Testament, prophets were often referred to as seers. This derives from the propensity of prophets to experience visions. Visions belong in the class of spiritual information known as revelation, generally imparted to us by the Holy Spirit through the manifestation gifts

[253] Frank B. Gill, *Ornithology*, W. H. Freeman & Co., New York, 1990, p. 160.

[254] The Wilson Bulletin—No. 100, https://sora.unm.edu/sites/default/files/journals/wilson/v029n03/p0164-p0165.pdf (accessed November 26, 2017).

[255] Susan Hagen, "The Mind's Eye," *Rochester Review* 74, no. 4 (2012): 35, http://www.rochester.edu/pr/Review/V74N4/0402_brainscience.html (accessed November 26, 2017).

[256] Joe Van Wormer, *Eagles*, Lodestar Books, E. P. Dutton, New York, 1985, p. 5.

of word of knowledge, word of wisdom, and discerning of spirits.[257] Through the eagle, the Holy Spirit demonstrates to us His extraordinary vision which He imparts to us by His grace.

While doves need to bob their heads to build depth perception, the eagle's eyes are set forward enough to provide them with binocular vision and extraordinary depth perception.[258] An eagle can spot a rabbit from two miles away.[259] As the dove's sight exemplifies our close and intimate relationship with the Holy Spirit, the eagle's vision speaks to us of the far-reaching prophetic view only He can provide to the saints.

Covenant and Covering

Like doves, eagles mate for life.[260] Jesus promised to never leave nor forsake us.[261] His surety of this promise is the ever-abiding, inward anointing of the Holy Spirit granted to the saints.[262] The Spirit seals us to redemption.

2 Corinthians 1:21-22
21 Now He who establishes us with you in Christ and has anointed us is God,
22 who also has sealed us and given us the Spirit in our hearts as a guarantee. NKJV

Eagles usually lay a clutch of two eggs, each of which are about twice the size of a chicken egg.[263] The female does most of the incubating, while the male supplies the food.[264] Once again, we see demonstrated in nature the cooperative efforts of the church and the Holy Spirit in

---

[257] 1 Cor. 12:7-10; Eph. 1:17-19.
[258] Wormer, p. 12.
[259] Switzer, p. 25.
[260] Wormer, p. 22.
[261] Heb. 13:5.
[262] 1 John 2:27.
[263] Wormer, p. 24.
[264] Ibid.

discipling new believers. During this crucial incubation period, the male patrols the nesting area to keep threats at bay and feeds its mate.[265]

In the parable of the sower, Jesus taught us that the enemy actively seeks to interfere with the growth of the gospel in people's hearts. His interpretation of the parable brought focus on the condition and reaction of the hearer's heart. The other dynamic in this cultivation of the heart is the Holy Spirit's protection of the saints.

Revelation 12:13-14
13 And when the dragon saw that he was cast unto the earth, he persecuted the woman which brought forth the man child.
14 And to the woman were given two wings of a great eagle, that she might fly into the wilderness, into her place, where she is nourished for a time, and times, and half a time, from the face of the serpent.

When we are receptive to the gifts that the Holy Spirit grants us, He provides us with the means to fly away from the serpent's face and find safe haven. Golden eagles prefer to nest in rocky cliffs.[266] The prophetic picture in Revelation and the golden eagles' preferred home both speak to us of the Holy Spirit carrying us to the safety of the Rock of our salvation.

Psalm 61:1-4
1 Hear my cry, O God; attend unto my prayer.
2 From the end of the earth will I cry unto thee, when my heart is overwhelmed: lead me to the rock that is higher than I.
3 For thou hast been a shelter for me, and a strong tower from the enemy.

---

[265] Sattler, p. 21.
[266] Wormer, p. 21.

4 I will abide in thy tabernacle for ever: I will trust in the covert of thy wings. Selah.

Once hatched, the eaglets enjoy the continual shade and warmth of their parent's wings. Gazing at the tiny hatchlings under the giant wingspan of the golden eagle paints a dramatic picture for us of our comparative weakness and size under the mighty wings of the Holy Spirit. May we continually abide under His covenant shadow while He renews our strength, so that we may run and not grow weary and walk without fainting.

CHAPTER 9

The Cloud
Wind, water, and fire leading the way

A cloud is essentially water vapor suspended in the air. Because of this, much of what we learned from the symbol of water is present in the cloud. But its significance goes beyond water, because the cloud the Holy Spirit used to symbolize Himself in Scripture is a particular type of cloud which, along with water, incorporates the dynamics of wind, as well as fire from heaven. Referred to as the *Shekhinah* in Talmudic writing,[267] its prominent presence in Scripture and what it teaches us about the Spirit warrant an examination of this symbol in its own right. It also is a topic that Scripture encourages us to be knowledgeable about.

1 Corinthians 10:1
Moreover, brethren, I would not that ye should be ignorant, how that all our fathers were under the cloud, and all passed through the sea;

Paul's reference takes us back to the exodus from Egypt.

Establishing the Symbol
Exodus 13:18, 21-22
18 But God led the people about, through the way of the wilderness of the Red sea: and the children of Israel went up harnessed out of the land of Egypt.

---

[267] Arthur Green, *These Are the Words: A Vocabulary of Jewish Spiritual Life*, Jewish Lights Publishing, Woodstock, 1999, p. 33.

*21 And the Lord went before them by day in a pillar of a cloud, to lead
them the way; and by night in a pillar of fire, to give them light; to
go by day and night:*

*22 He took not away the pillar of the cloud by day, nor the pillar of
fire by night, from before the people.*

God led His people in the pillar of cloud and pillar of fire. These were
not two different pillars. They were the same wonder that took on a
different appearance depending on the time of day and is an example
of the incarnational nature of Biblical revelation.

When caravans traveled in the days of the patriarchs, those in the lead
would carry small iron vessels or grates with wood fires burning in
them, fixed on long poles. The smoke of these fires would help guide
those in the rear of the caravan during the day, and the fire would
show them the direction at night.[268] The Lord embraced this cultural
reality when He appeared to lead the way through the covenant for
Abram. He then amplified this appearance through the pillar of cloud
and fire when He led the children of Israel out of Egypt. When He
came to formalize the covenant at Sinai, He did so in the awesome
manifestation of the Cloud.

Exodus 19:16-20

*16 And it came to pass on the third day in the morning, that there were
thunders and lightnings, and a thick cloud upon the mount, and the
voice of the trumpet exceeding loud; so that all the people that was
in the camp trembled.*

*17 And Moses brought forth the people out of the camp to meet with
God; and they stood at the nether part of the mount.*

*18 And mount Sinai was altogether on a smoke, because the Lord de-
scended upon it in fire: and the smoke thereof ascended as the
smoke of a furnace, and the whole mount quaked greatly.*

---

[268] *PC Study Bible: The New Unger's Bible Dictionary*, "Pillar of Cloud and Fire," Originally published by Moody Press, Chicago, 1988.

19 And when the voice of the trumpet sounded long, and waxed louder and louder, Moses spake, and God answered him by a voice.

20 And the Lord came down upon mount Sinai, on the top of the mount: and the Lord called Moses up to the top of the mount; and Moses went up.

If you are used to imagining the pillar of cloud as a peaceful puff of smoke drifting before the departing Israelites, the verses above should be a revelation. In the natural, the type of thick cloud that gives birth to thunder and lightning is the *cumulonimbus capillatus*, the anvil-headed thundercloud—the very same type of cloud that spawns tornadoes. This is the true picture of what the children of Israel followed through the wilderness for forty years: an anvil-headed thunder cloud with a tornado reaching the ground that flashed with heaven's fire at night to light the way.

Psalm 77:17-20

17 The clouds poured out water; the skies gave forth thunder; your arrows flashed on every side.

18 The crash of your thunder was in the whirlwind; your lightnings lighted up the world; the earth trembled and shook.

19 Your way was through the sea, your path through the great waters; yet your footprints were unseen.

20 You led your people like a flock by the hand of Moses and Aaron. ESV

The *Shekhinah* and its pillar that connected heaven and earth was not a natural thunderstorm. But its appearance took on that form. Meteorologists classify highly organized thunderstorms that live longer than an hour a "supercell." The picture below (Figure 9.1) may give the reader some idea of the magnitude of the cloud and its pillar that led the children of Israel.

Figure 9.1

Overshooting top

Anvil

Cumulonimbus

Flanking Line

Wall Cloud

Rain and/or Hail

Tornado

NOAA

These storms can be as large as 10 miles in diameter and rise up to 50,000 feet high. Notice how small the tornado is in proportion to the cloud that births it. Once again our attention is drawn to scale, to the immense size of the supply in proportion to the outpouring.

So, let's consider the Exodus passage a second time, having understood the magnitude of the pillar of cloud and fire:

Exodus 13:18, 21-22
18 But God led the people about, through the way of the wilderness of the Red sea: and the children of Israel went up harnessed out of the land of Egypt.
21 And the Lord went before them by day in a pillar of a cloud, to lead them the way; and by night in a pillar of fire, to give them light; to go by day and night:
22 He took not away the pillar of the cloud by day, nor the pillar of fire by night, from before the people.

When we pair these verses with other descriptions of the event, we can see the association of the Holy Spirit with this mighty sign from God.

Isaiah 63:11-14

11 Then he remembered the days of old, of Moses and his people. Where is he who brought them up out of the sea with the shepherds of his flock? Where is he who put in the midst of them his Holy Spirit,

12 who caused his glorious arm to go at the right hand of Moses, who divided the waters before them to make for himself an everlasting name,

13 who led them through the depths? Like a horse in the desert, they did not stumble.

14 Like livestock that go down into the valley, the Spirit of the Lord gave them rest. So you led your people, to make for yourself a glorious name. ESV

While Exodus highlights the Cloud's leading of God's people, Isaiah centers on the Spirit's presence in the event. The children of Israel mentioned both in their praises to God during their days of recommitment to the covenant under Nehemiah's leadership.

Nehemiah 9:19-20

19 you in your great mercies did not forsake them in the wilderness. The pillar of cloud to lead them in the way did not depart from them by day, nor the pillar of fire by night to light for them the way by which they should go.

20 You gave your good Spirit to instruct them and did not withhold your manna from their mouth and gave them water for their thirst. ESV

It is encouraging to know that God in His great mercy does not abandon us to our sin. The writer of Hebrews reminds us that the Lord will never leave us nor forsake us.[269] Despite the blasphemy of the golden calf (Neh. 9:18), God stayed in Israel's midst in the abiding presence

---

[269] Heb. 13:5.

of His Spirit as manifested in the pillar of cloud and fire. In writing to the Corinthian church, Paul further solidifies this connection.

1 Corinthians 10:1b-4
1 ... all our fathers were under the cloud, and all passed through the sea;
2 And were all baptized unto Moses in the cloud and in the sea;
3 And did all eat the same spiritual meat;
4 And did all drink the same spiritual drink: for they drank of that spiritual Rock that followed them: and that Rock was Christ.

Paul showed that the Red Sea crossing was a baptismal event involving two distinct means of immersion: the cloud and the sea. He then revealed that the waters of Maribah went beyond the mere slaking of the people's thirst. The Israelites tempted the Lord with their contentious questioning. "Is the Lord among us or not," they asked. God's response was to pour out water from the stricken Rock.[270] This event prefigured the piercing of Jesus's side, from which poured out blood and water.[271] Where His blood is poured, the Spirit follows. Because of Christ's sacrifice, the Holy Spirit is able to take up permanent habitation in us. In the space of four verses, Paul crosses the Red Sea, journeys into the wilderness, climbs Sinai and Calvary, and drinks from the Rock, Pentecost's spiritual fountain.[272] Later in the letter, he states his case even more concisely.

1 Corinthians 12:13
For by one Spirit are we all baptized into one body, whether we be Jews or Gentiles, whether we be bond or free; and have been all made to drink into one Spirit.

"For by one Spirit are we all baptized into one body" answers to "all baptized unto Moses in the cloud." The cloud baptism spoke of Holy

---

[270] Exod. 17:3-7.
[271] John 19:34.
[272] Acts 2:33.

Spirit baptism even as the sea baptism spoke of water baptism. These scriptures, taken as a whole, establish the cloud as a symbol of the Holy Spirit. The Spirit progressively revealed the reality of the cloud as redemption's plan unfolded through the Scriptures.

The Progressive Revelation of the Cloud

The Holy Spirit teaches us about the Shekinah Cloud through progressive revelation in the Bible. Conner and Malmin define progressive revelation as "the successive unfolding of a continuous theme to its consummation ... These themes in Scripture can be symbolized as 'rivers of truth' that begin in Genesis and run through the books of the Bible into the 'sea' of Revelation. God did not give the full truth at once; rather, He unfolded it progressively to man step by step, detail by detail, each portion giving further amplification and clarification."[273]

Manfred Brauch states that progressive revelation results from the incarnational nature of Scripture. God's Word came to us within the confines of human language and within the context of human history. Its ultimate incarnation was in the Person of Jesus of Nazareth. He contends that disregarding this truth leads to abusing the context of Scripture.[274] With regard to "progressive revelation" or the "progressive unfolding" of God's revelation, he writes:

"These terms communicate the truth that God did not reveal the totality of his redemptive project to Israel in its infancy. New and deeper truths about God, about the human reality of alienation from God, and about God's purposes for dealing with that alienation were disclosed to and through God's servants in subsequent stages of redemptive history."[275]

---

[273] Kevin J. Conner and Ken Malmin, *Interpreting the Scriptures*, Bible Temple Publishing, Portland, 1983, p. 65.
[274] Manfred T. Brauch, *Abusing Scripture: The Consequences of Misreading the Bible*, InterVarsity Press, Downers Grove, 2009, pp. 25, 202-203.
[275] Brauch, p. 203.

As Isaiah wrote, "For precept must be upon precept, precept upon precept; line upon line, line upon line; here a little, and there a little."[276] It is in just such a manner that God moves from appearing as smoke from a smoldering pot to cloven tongues of fire to teach us about His abiding presence within us through the Holy Spirit.

The Covenant that Prefigured the Cloud

Genesis 15:9-10, 17-18a

9 So He said to him, "Bring Me a three-year-old heifer, a three-year-old female goat, a three-year-old ram, a turtledove, and a young pigeon."

10 Then he brought all these to Him and cut them in two, down the middle, and placed each piece opposite the other; but he did not cut the birds in two.

17 And it came to pass, when the sun went down and it was dark, that behold, there appeared a smoking oven and a burning torch that passed between those pieces.

18 On the same day the Lord made a covenant with Abram ... NKJV

We looked at this narrative briefly in Chapter 7 when we noted that doves were not divided like other sacrificial animals. In the ceremony of cutting covenant, the two parties would walk through the pieces of the divided animals signifying the consequence to either of not keeping the covenant. By walking through the blood of the butchered beasts, covenant makers were proclaiming, "May I be like one of these slaughtered animals should I fail to deliver on my promise." This covenant was unique in that it was unilateral. The Lord alone walked through the blood in the form of smoke and fire and made a promise to Himself about what He would do for Abram and all his children. In this way, God made the covenant unbreakable because it is impossible for Him to lie.

---

[276] Isa. 28:9-12 with 1 Cor. 14:21-22.

Hebrews 6:13-14, 17-18

13 For when God made promise to Abraham, because he could swear by no greater, he sware by himself,

14 Saying, Surely blessing I will bless thee, and multiplying I will multiply thee.

17 Wherein God, willing more abundantly to shew unto the heirs of promise the immutability of his counsel, confirmed it by an oath:

18 That by two immutable things, in which it was impossible for God to lie, we might have a strong consolation, who have fled for refuge to lay hold upon the hope set before us:

The smoking pot and a burning torch prefigured the pillar of cloud and fire that appeared to lead the children of Israel out of Egypt after the Passover event. His appearance in the form of a smoking and fiery brazier is another great example of the incarnational nature of biblical revelation. The Cloud's appearance at Abram's sacrifice, Passover's exit, and Sinai's encounter speak to us of the Holy Spirit as the Spirit of promise and covenant.

Jeremiah 31:31-34

31 Behold, the days come, saith the Lord, that I will make a new covenant with the house of Israel, and with the house of Judah:

32 Not according to the covenant that I made with their fathers in the day that I took them by the hand to bring them out of the land of Egypt; which my covenant they brake, although I was an husband unto them, saith the Lord:

*33 But this shall be the covenant that I will make with the house of Israel; After those days, saith the Lord, **I will put my law in their inward parts, and write it in their hearts**; and will be their God, and they shall be my people.* [Emphasis added.]

34 And they shall teach no more every man his neighbour, and every man his brother, saying, Know the Lord: for they shall all know me, from the least of them unto the greatest of them, saith the Lord; for I will forgive their iniquity, and I will remember their sin no more.

Paul takes up the theme of verse 33 in his second letter to the saints in Corinth when he declares them to be the epistle of Christ written in the heart by the Spirit of the living God.[277] John, resonating with verse 34, wrote:

1 John 2:27
But the anointing which ye have received of him abideth in you, and ye need not that any man teach you: but as the same anointing teacheth you of all things, and is truth, and is no lie, and even as it hath taught you, ye shall abide in him.

When the Holy Spirit established His residence in our hearts, He sealed the new covenant in our spirits, changing us from children of disobedience to new creations in Christ who are predisposed to doing the will of God.

The Cloud of Communion
Every healthy relationship has ground rules and boundaries. The ground rules establish how we interact with one another, and the boundaries define what is outside the realm of healthy interaction. When we cross the boundaries, we breach the relationship. God establishes ground rules and boundaries through covenant. The purpose of covenant is to provide communion. It is fitting then that along with being present at covenant making, the Cloud is also a place of communion.

Exodus 19:9
And the Lord said unto Moses, Lo, I come unto thee in a thick cloud, that the people may hear when I speak with thee, and believe thee for ever. And Moses told the words of the people unto the Lord.

The Lord came to Moses in a thick cloud and spoke to him. His manifest presence in communing with Moses continued well after the Mount Sinai experience.

---

[277] 2 Cor. 3:3.

Exodus 33:7-11

7 *And Moses took the tabernacle, and pitched it without the camp, afar off from the camp, and called it the Tabernacle of the congregation. And it came to pass, that every one which sought the Lord went out unto the tabernacle of the congregation, which was without the camp.*

8 *And it came to pass, when Moses went out unto the tabernacle, that all the people rose up, and stood every man at his tent door, and looked after Moses, until he was gone into the tabernacle.*

9 *And it came to pass, as Moses entered into the tabernacle, the cloudy pillar descended, and stood at the door of the tabernacle, and the Lord talked with Moses.*

10 *And all the people saw the cloudy pillar stand at the tabernacle door: and all the people rose up and worshipped, every man in his tent door.*

11 *And the Lord spake unto Moses face to face, as a man speaketh unto his friend.*

The tent Moses set up outside the camp was not the tabernacle sanctuary, for its fabrication was yet future. The "outside" tent was a regular tent Moses erected to meet with God. The Lord graced it with His presence, meeting him there in the Cloud. But God had no intention of remaining *outside* of the camp.

Exodus 25:8
And let them make me a sanctuary; that I may dwell among them.

The Lord's intent has always been to dwell *among* His people. Once the tabernacle and its furnishings were built and set up, the Israelites were instructed to camp around it. The Lord's tent—His dwelling— was in the center of the encampment.[278] Though this sanctuary was more substantial than Moses's tent, its purpose was the same. It was

---

[278] Num. 1-4.

the community's place of fellowship with God. It was the place where the Cloud came to rest.

Exodus 40:33-38

33 And he reared up the court round about the tabernacle and the altar, and set up the hanging of the court gate. So Moses finished the work.

34 Then a cloud covered the tent of the congregation, and the glory of the Lord filled the tabernacle.

35 And Moses was not able to enter into the tent of the congregation, because the cloud abode thereon, and the glory of the Lord filled the tabernacle.

36 And when the cloud was taken up from over the tabernacle, the children of Israel went onward in all their journeys:

37 But if the cloud were not taken up, then they journeyed not till the day that it was taken up.

38 For the cloud of the Lord was upon the tabernacle by day, and fire was on it by night, in the sight of all the house of Israel, throughout all their journeys.

The Cloud not only signified God's dwelling; it also indicated His movement. Communion starts in the camp, but deepens in a shared journey. As the prophet said, two walk together when they are in agreement.[279] Just as the children of Israel followed the Cloud in their wilderness wanderings, we are to follow the Holy Spirit in our walk through this life. It is only through obediently following His lead that we are set free from the lusts of the flesh and the bondage of the law to walk in the fruitful freedom that Christ purchased for us on the cross.[280]

The Cloud of Glory

Moses watched as the Cloud covered the tabernacle on its inauguration

---

[279] Amos 3:3.
[280] Gal. 4-5.

day and wrote that "the glory of the Lord filled the tabernacle," thus equating the Cloud's appearance with the splendor and majesty of God's presence. King Solomon acknowledged the same truth when the ark of the covenant was placed in the holy of holies of the temple. The Cloud descended on the house of the Lord and His glory filled it, causing Solomon to declare, "The Lord said that he would dwell in a dark cloud."[281] The glory cloud is substantial and weighty, ominous and awe inspiring. What Moses and Solomon observed in the natural on earth, Isaiah saw in a spiritual glimpse of the heavenlies.

Isaiah 6:1-4

1 In the year that king Uzziah died I saw also the Lord sitting upon a throne, high and lifted up, and his train filled the temple.

2 Above it stood the seraphims: each one had six wings; with twain he covered his face, and with twain he covered his feet, and with twain he did fly.

3 And one cried unto another, and said, Holy, holy, holy, is the Lord of hosts: the whole earth is full of his glory.

4 And the posts of the door moved at the voice of him that cried, and the house was filled with smoke.

Isaiah's glimpse of God's glory filled him with gloom, for in God's holy light he recognized how truly unclean and worthy of death he was. It is the holiness of God that imbues the Cloud with weight. No mortal can move under its mantle. The prophet's cry is our own when we see ourselves in relation to God's holiness. We are woefully undone.

Isaiah 6:5-7

5 Then said I, Woe is me! for I am undone; because I am a man of unclean lips, and I dwell in the midst of a people of unclean lips: for mine eyes have seen the King, the Lord of hosts.

6 Then flew one of the seraphims unto me, having a live coal in his

---

[281] 1 Kings 8:6-12 NKJV (compare with Deut. 4:10-12).

hand, which he had taken with the tongs from off the altar:

7 And he laid it upon my mouth, and said, Lo, this hath touched thy lips; and thine iniquity is taken away, and thy sin purged.

How is it possible for a glowing ember to purge sin? The coals on the altar resulted from heaven's fire. The Lord lit the wood under the sacrifice. As the offering burned, its blood dripped down and was vaporized in the heat sending a column of smoke upward. All altars speak of sacrifice, and all sacrifices point to Jesus on the cross. The smoke and the fire that freed Isaiah from the filth of his sin speak to us of the Spirit imparting to us the finished work of Christ through the Cloud.

Leviticus 9:22-24

22 And Aaron lifted up his hand toward the people, and blessed them, and came down from offering of the sin offering, and the burnt offering, and peace offerings.

23 And Moses and Aaron went into the tabernacle of the congregation, and came out, and blessed the people: and the glory of the Lord appeared unto all the people.

24 And there came a fire out from before the Lord, and consumed upon the altar the burnt offering and the fat: which when all the people saw, they shouted, and fell on their faces.

"The glory of the Lord appeared unto all the people," tells us that the Cloud was in full manifestation. "And there came a fire out from before the Lord," describes the fire of heaven—holy lightning incinerating the sacred offering. While the spiritual *Shekinah* gave visible witness of the Lord's presence in the cloud and power in the lightning, fire burned in the natural and a column of smoke rose to heaven. In the Cloud, the Holy Spirit teaches us that Christ's sacrifice was accepted. Our iniquity is taken away and our sins are purged. This is the glory of the Lord reflected in us.

2 Corinthians 3:17-18

17 Now the Lord is that Spirit: and where the Spirit of the Lord is, there is liberty.

18 But we all, with open face beholding as in a glass the glory of the Lord, are changed into the same image from glory to glory, even as by the Spirit of the Lord.

Wonders in the Whirlwind

Ezekiel 1:1-3

1 Now it came to pass in the thirtieth year, in the fourth month, in the fifth day of the month, as I was among the captives by the river of Chebar, that the heavens were opened, and I saw visions of God.

2 In the fifth day of the month, which was the fifth year of king Jehoi-achin's captivity,

3 The word of the Lord came expressly unto Ezekiel the priest, the son of Buzi, in the land of the Chaldeans by the river Chebar; and the hand of the Lord was there upon him.

Many of the prophets had day jobs. Joseph and Daniel were in government. Samuel worked as a priest. Amos was a shepherd, as was Abel. Ezekiel was a priest, but he was far from the establishment of his employment, so I am unsure of what his day job might have been. When I read the above, I like to imagine him fishing, even though he was probably farming. I can see him standing on the bank of the wide irrigation canal hoping to catch something extra for dinner when a stiff breeze makes him look up to a sight that would motivate anyone who grew up in Tornado Alley to run for the cellar.

Ezekiel 1:4

And I looked, and, behold, a whirlwind came out of the north, a great cloud, and a fire infolding itself, and a brightness was about it, and out of the midst thereof as the colour of amber, out of the midst of the fire.

If we read no farther, we could stay safely in Kansas—or in my case Arkansas, which was the portion of the Alley I grew up in. If you have ever watched a massive thunderstorm move in, particularly in the late afternoon, you have seen this mighty wind-and-water engine driving forward in massive electrical displays of flashing fire. The density of the storm and the setting sun turn it to burnished amber with promises of sulfuric fury. Once one spots the funnel cloud reaching down in full tornadic turbulence, it's best to find a hole in the ground. One has to admire Ezekiel. He didn't dive into the canal. He stood his ground and kept looking.

Ezekiel 1:5-8
5 Also out of the midst thereof came the likeness of four living crea-
  tures. And this was their appearance; they had the likeness of a man.
6 And every one had four faces, and every one had four wings.
7 And their feet were straight feet; and the sole of their feet was like
  the sole of a calf's foot: and they sparkled like the colour of bur-
  nished brass.
8 And they had the hands of a man under their wings on their four
  sides; and they four had their faces and their wings.

As the prophet peers through the fiery mist of the storm, the forms of the living creatures appear, rolling across the plain on wheels full of eyes and fire. Undaunted, Ezekiel continues to carry his gaze upward.

Ezekiel 1:22
And the likeness of the firmament upon the heads of the living creature was as the colour of the terrible crystal, stretched forth over their heads above.

A crystal firmament crowned the heads of the living creatures. The apostle John saw this firmament as well, but from his perspective it was the floor of heaven. He described it as a "sea of glass like crystal"[282] upon which sat the throne of God.

Revelation 4:3-5

3 And he that sat was to look upon like a jasper and a sardine stone: and there was a rainbow round about the throne, in sight like unto an emerald.

4 And round about the throne were four and twenty seats: and upon the seats I saw four and twenty elders sitting, clothed in white raiment; and they had on their heads crowns of gold.

5 And out of the throne proceeded lightnings and thunderings and voices: and there were seven lamps of fire burning before the throne, which are the seven Spirits of God.

We examined these Scriptures while learning about the Holy Spirit as fire (Chapter 4) and as the lamp (Chapter 6). Here in the Cloud, we see these symbols coming together as we get glimpses beyond the veil. What John stood before, Ezekiel sees above him.

Ezekiel 1:26-28

26 And above the firmament that was over their heads was the likeness of a throne, as the appearance of a sapphire stone: and upon the likeness of the throne was the likeness as the appearance of a man above upon it.

27 And I saw as the colour of amber, as the appearance of fire round about within it, from the appearance of his loins even upward, and from the appearance of his loins even downward, I saw as it were the appearance of fire, and it had brightness round about.

28 As the appearance of the bow that is in the cloud in the day of rain, so was the appearance of the brightness round about. This was the appearance of the likeness of the glory of the Lord. And when I saw it, I fell upon my face, and I heard a voice of one that spake.

---

[282] Rev. 4:6.

The living creatures constitute the chariot of God.[283] The chariot and the throne that sits above it are shrouded in the Cloud. The Creator gives us a view of this supernatural reality every time clouds coalesce into a supercell thunderstorm.

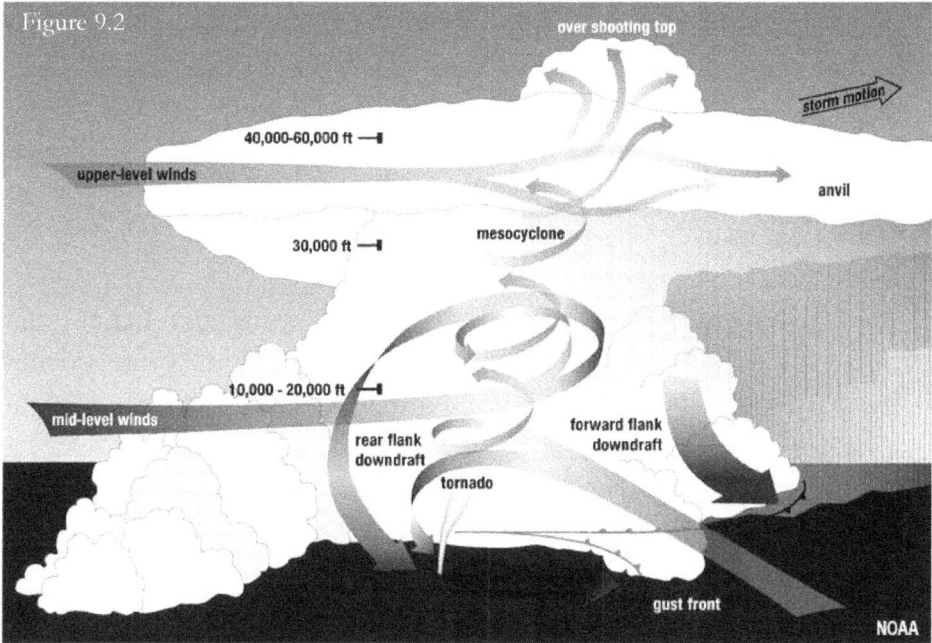

Figure 9.2

The diagram above (Figure 9.2) illustrates the wind dynamics that frame the shape of the cloud. We can map the spiritual realities the Holy Spirit has taught us through symbolism on all the natural components of the supercell. The warm air updrafts that feed the cell through its updraft core and culminate in the over-shooting top or stratospheric dome represent the praises God inhabits. The dome curves end-to-end on the tropopause, the boundary between the troposphere and the stratosphere. As the warm air moves upward, it cools and condenses to form the cloud. The shearing winds of the upper troposphere flatten the cloud which at 40,000-60,000 feet has encountered air chilly enough to crystalize it. This is "the sea of glass like crystal" in the natural.

---

[283] Ps. 18:6-14; 104:1-3.

The collision of all those water molecules polarizes the cloud with a net positive charge at its top and a net negative charge at the bottom. The charge separation over thousands of feet produces millions of volts of electrical potential. Once this potential overcomes the resistance in the air, lightning flashes its way down to earth, heating the atmosphere around it three times hotter than the surface of the Sun. Fire has come down from heaven, and the voice of God thunders.

The air cools and pressurizes as it travels upward. It makes its way back to earth in cold downdrafts that remind us of the times of refreshing brought to us by the wind of the Spirit. Rain and hail fall from the cloud, speaking to us of the Spirit's outpouring, as well as His conviction in judgment. As the storm gusts forward, colliding wind currents twist around each other and funnel down to earth in a tornado that clears a path on the ground, leaving a roadmap of the direction of the storm for all to follow. The pillar of cloud has appeared to lead the way for all those watching. I have relabeled the supercell diagram below (Figure 9.3) to illustrate some of these truths.

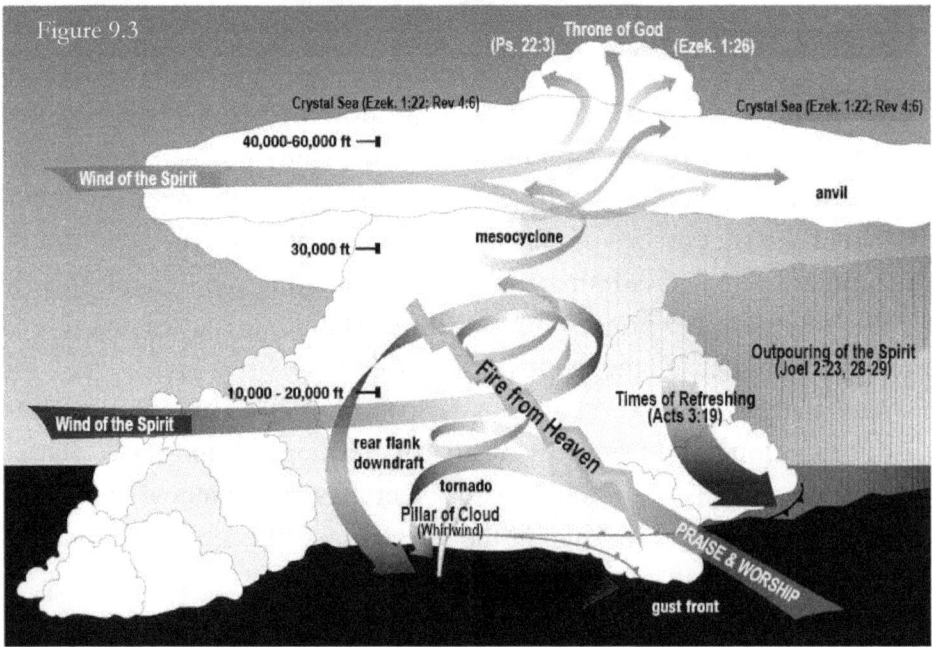

Figure 9.3

Throne of God (Ps. 22:3) (Ezek. 1:26)

Crystal Sea (Ezek. 1:22; Rev 4:6)

Crystal Sea (Ezek. 1:22; Rev 4:6)

40,000-60,000 ft

Wind of the Spirit

anvil

mesocyclone

30,000 ft

Outpouring of the Spirit (Joel 2:23, 28-29)

10,000 - 20,000 ft

Fire from Heaven

Times of Refreshing (Acts 3:19)

Wind of the Spirit

rear flank downdraft

tornado

Pillar of Cloud (Whirlwind)

PRAISE & WORSHIP

gust front

The Cloud and the Church

On the day of Pentecost, the roar of the whirlwind filled the Temple as the Holy Spirit appeared in the pillar of fire with flames reaching out to rest upon the apostles' heads to let them know that the promise of the Father had come.[284] Filled with the abiding presence of the Spirit, they brought forth for the first time the New Testament manifestation of speaking in tongues. In response to the questions and mocking, Peter rose to his feet with his companions and delivered what is arguably his best-known sermon.

Acts 2:17-19

17 "'In the last days, God says, I will pour out my Spirit on all people. Your sons and daughters will prophesy, your young men will see visions, your old men will dream dreams.

18 Even on my servants, both men and women, I will pour out my Spirit in those days, and they will prophesy.

19 I will show wonders in the heaven above and signs on the earth below, blood and fire and billows of smoke. NIV

"Blood and fire and billows of smoke," bring us all the way back to Abraham's vision of the Lord making His way through the sacrifice as a burning torch and a smoking furnace. The Holy Spirit appeared in the rushing sound and flashing fire of the Shekinah cloud in response to the perfect blood of the now-glorified Christ poured out in sacrifice for the sins of mankind.[285] Even as the Cloud appeared at the dedication of the tabernacle and the temple, it was present when the true temple of the Holy Spirit had its foundation stones set.[286] His fire still burns within us, causing billows of intercession and worship to rise to the Father in heaven. He moves us ever forward into the presence of God, reaping the fields white for harvest that grow in response to His rains of grace.

---

[284] Luke 24:49. See also Chapter 4 – Fire under the section "Fire and Sacrifice."

[285] John 7:36-37; Acts 2:33; Heb. 9:11-15.

[286] Eph. 2:18-22; 1 Cor. 6:19-20.

Isaiah 45:8

Rain down, you heavens, from above, And let the skies pour down righteousness; Let the earth open, let them bring forth salvation, And let righteousness spring up together. I, the Lord, have created it. NKJV

CHAPTER 10

Conclusion: The Language of Symbol
The Creator's communication to His creatures

When God made Adam, He imparted spirit life into a clay jar inten-tionally. He placed us—sentient beings with spirit life—in a material creation to experience a relationship with Him unlike any relationship He had with any of His creatures before. Angels were created as in-habitants in a spiritual realm, but we were created in the material realm to become a habitation of God through the Spirit. Our physical architecture—the very thing that made the Incarnation possible—makes us blind to the realities of the spirit realm. Instead of allowing this physical barrier to become an excuse for unbelief, God fully en-gaged it. He called us to peer into His creation to perceive that which our eyes could not see—His eternal power and Godhead. He did this through the language of symbol.

Romans 1:20
For his invisible attributes, namely, his eternal power and divine na-ture, have been clearly perceived, ever since the creation of the world, in the things that have been made. So they are without excuse. ESV

We return to where we began this study: the Lord's expression of Himself in the created order. To help us appreciate the importance of the principle of symbolism in Scripture, I have enlisted the help of the teacher of teachers, the Master Himself, the Lord Jesus.

John 3:1-3
1 Now there was a man of the Pharisees named Nicodemus, a ruler of the Jews.

2 This man came to Jesus by night and said to him, "Rabbi, we know that you are a teacher come from God, for no one can do these signs that you do unless God is with him."

3 Jesus answered him, "Truly, truly, I say to you, unless one is born again he cannot see the kingdom of God." ESV

Nicodemus, a prominent Pharisee and member of the Sanhedrin, comes in the obscurity of the night to seek audience with the audacious and controversial rabbi from the Galilee. He compliments Jesus, certifying him as "a teacher come from God" because he does miracles. Jesus's response is such a non sequitur that it risks hitting my funny bone. Imagine for a minute that Fred, vice president of the homeowners association, approaches his new neighbor Bill about his garden. He wants to learn from the newcomer but isn't too keen on the rest of the yard monitors knowing about it. So, one late afternoon he makes his way over to the fence and—perhaps the illustration below (Figure 10.1) would do this more justice.

Figure 10.1

Once approached, Jesus takes complete command of the conversation. Nicodemus was talking about miraculously-approved godly teachers (Fred's compliment in the cartoon above) and Jesus responds with the requirement for seeing the kingdom of God (Bill's response to his neighbor's compliment). If I was Nicodemus—which I am not, I'm Nikolas—I would be scratching my head. Although John doesn't give us any action clues in this narrative to illustrate Nicodemus's disorientation, his documentation of the conversation does give us a clear sense of the Pharisee's cognitive whiplash.

John 3:4
Nicodemus said to him, "How can a man be born when he is old? Can he enter a second time into his mother's womb and be born?" ESV

All of Nicodemus's strategies and concerns have been preempted by Jesus's proclamation. "You're a great teacher," says Nicodemus. "You need a rebirth," Jesus replies. "What are you talking about? I'm a grown man. How does a grown man crawl back into his mother's womb and make his way back out again? You are not making sense!" If you are like me, you read this with a bit of a knowing smile, like someone who is in on the punch line. But are we?

Nicodemus and Jesus share the same language, the same culture, and the same time frame. These are all barriers we must leap to appreciate the setting of this narrative. To do so, we read words translated by scholars who speak our language and commentaries written within the last two hundred years to help us gather the cultural context of an interchange that occurred in a bubble of time over two thousand years ago. Are we smug enough to believe we have a full sense of what Jesus is saying when His contemporary was left grasping for straws? Or do we really believe Nicodemus was too dull to perceive the Master's true intent? Might there be mystery left yet in the Master's message?

John 3:5-10
5 Jesus answered, "Truly, truly, I say to you, unless one is born of water and the Spirit, he cannot enter the kingdom of God.
6 That which is born of the flesh is flesh, and that which is born of the Spirit is spirit.
7 Do not marvel that I said to you, 'You must be born again.'

*8 The wind blows where it wishes, and you hear its sound, but you do
not know where it comes from or where it goes. So it is with every-
one who is born of the Spirit."*

9 Nicodemus said to him, "How can these things be?"

*10 Jesus answered him, "Are you the teacher of Israel and yet you do
not understand these things? ESV*

Jesus expounds on His statement for Nicodemus's benefit and ours.
He tells him of being born of water (natural birth and baptism) and the
Spirit (baptism and spiritual birth). He applies the lessons of creation
from Genesis (everything after its kind) telling him that flesh births
flesh and Spirit births spirit. "Don't be surprised by the requirement of
rebirth," Jesus tells him. "Are you shocked or surprised that the wind
blows where and when it wants and though you hear it, you don't
know where it came from or where it's going? Spirit children are just
like that."

"How can these things be?" Nicodemus asks. How, indeed. How does
one become a Spirit child? How can they sound like the breeze, move
like the wind, and be invisible? How is all this possible? "You're a
teacher and you don't understand these things?" the Master asks. Jesus
has exposed Nicodemus to his ignorance and need. The man who
complimented the Master as an instructor sent from God has his own
credentials examined and found deficient. His ways are not our ways,
and His thoughts are above our thoughts. It is only when we
acknowledge this reality that our minds begin to thaw and become pli-
able in the hands of Truth.

John 3:11-12

*11 Truly, truly, I say to you, we speak of what we know, and bear wit-
ness to what we have seen, but you do not receive our testimony.*

*12 If I have told you earthly things and you do not believe, how can
you believe if I tell you heavenly things? ESV*

Even though Jesus t-boned Nicodemus's train of thought with His opening statement, He still speaks to him in context. "You are a teacher come from God," Nicodemus said. His "you" and "God" form the "we" of Jesus's testimony. "We speak what we know." The Godhead who cannot lie is talking. Jesus does not deal in theories or suppositions. He communicates ultimate reality as a first-hand witness. His testimony is infallible. What has He been talking about? Seeing the kingdom of God, being born again, entering God's kingdom, being a Spirit child that travels invisibly with undeniable impact—all these He calls "earthly things." For those of us who thought we knew what Jesus was talking about, our ignorance and need has been exposed. We should be asking with Nicodemus, "How can these things be? How can all these spiritual realities be *earthly things*?"

Jesus answered this question in response to a different query. The Master had just finished praying, and His disciples asked for instruction in heavenly communication. We know His answer as The Lord's Prayer.

Luke 11:2
And he said unto them, When ye pray, say, Our Father which art in heaven, Hallowed be thy name. Thy kingdom come. Thy will be done, as in heaven, so in earth.

Dragging the earthly to heaven isn't God's endgame. His desire is for heaven to come to earth, to creatures such as such us—creatures He crafted from the dust of the ground. His communication to us is thus continually colored with the language of creation, the language of earthly things. Jesus told Nicodemus about the work of the Spirit of God on the Earth and in man. Because the Spirit's work happens here, Jesus expressed the reality of it in condescending, earthly comparisons. The Spirit is invisible, but we have all felt the wind. Spiritual regeneration may seem an abstract ideal, but it has the same visceral validity as uterine contractions inexorably pressing one into the light of day for the first time. These earthly things must be believed to have faith to see the heavenly. Herein lies the importance of symbol.

The Language of Symbol in Creation

Having journeyed this far together, it is my sincere hope that the reader has seen the integrity with which the Holy Spirit has encoded His character in the creations He used to exemplify Himself. The symbolic principle of Biblical interpretation isn't arbitrary and fanciful. It follows solid rules of logic and remains consistent from Genesis through Revelation. Kevin Connor explains it in the following way:

> "A symbol [in Scripture] ... is designed to represent certain characteristics or qualities in that which it represents. To be interpreted, it requires a pointing out of the characteristics, qualities, marks or features **common** to both the symbol and that which it symbolizes."[287]

> "God, in authoring the Bible, dealt with both creation and redemption. The first two chapters of Genesis contain the record of creation of the natural realm [earthly things]: the rest of the Bible contains God's plan of redemption. In Scripture God uses the natural things He created to become symbols (Romans 1:19-20). In other words, **the language of creation becomes the language of symbol which in turn becomes the language of redemption**."[288]

In concluding this study, I felt it appropriate to use the Genesis creation narrative as a lens through which to review the symbols we have studied and perhaps gain additional insights into the Holy Spirit and His relationship with us.

---

[287] Kevin Connor, *Interpreting the Symbols and Types*, BT Publishing, Portland, OR, 1992, p. 85.
[288] Kevin Connor, Ken Malmin, *Interpreting the Scriptures*, BT Publishing, Portland, OR, 1983, p. 125, emphasis added.

Wind

Wind, which we experience as atmospheric motion and breathing, is present in the word "Spirit"—*ruwach*, "wind" in Hebrew—and appears prior to the creation of the firmament (atmosphere and space).[289] As such, it is shown as above and before the created order. The Lord called forth the firmament on the second day. Two is the number of witness and testimony in Scripture (Deut. 19:15). The Holy Spirit is the signing witness on our heavenly birth certificate.

Romans 8:16
The Spirit itself beareth witness with our spirit, that we are the children of God:

Along with being the number of witness and testimony, two is also the number of separation and division. The firmament formed on the second day separated the waters above from the waters below (Gen. 1:6-8). It is the wind of the Spirit that joins the waters above—the living water of the Godhead—with the waters below, the spirits of men. It also separates us from all that is not fruitful.

Matthew 3:11-12
11 I indeed baptize you with water unto repentance: but he that cometh after me is mightier than I, whose shoes I am not worthy to bear: he shall baptize you with the Holy Ghost, and with fire:
12 Whose fan is in his hand, and he will throughly purge his floor, and gather his wheat into the garner; but he will burn up the chaff with unquenchable fire.

Water

Water is present in Genesis 1:2 in the words "deep" and "waters." Narratively, then, it stands as uncreated and pervasively present. We understand that H_2O is created, since we know hydrogen and oxygen were created. But in the Bible, water shows up before the details of the

---

[289] Gen. 1:2.

creation story and, as such, represents the eternal uncreated. After dividing the waters with the firmament, God gathered those that were below and then began to call life out on the planet. Water is necessary for life, and the Spirit is the Water of Life.

Fire

Fire makes its debut on day one with the Lord's proclamation of "Let there be light."[290] A careful read of Genesis 1 reveals that all we associate with the bonfires of the universe—starlight and all its reflectors—shined into the ether for the first time on the fourth day when God said, "Let there be lights in the firmament of heaven to divide the day from the night."[291]

One is the number of the Godhead in Scripture, "Hear, O Israel: The Lord our God is **one** Lord" (Deut. 6:4, emphasis added). The Holy Spirit is the Spirit of Truth, who shines the light of revelation to dispel the darkness in our souls. Dividing day from night is only one of light's jobs.

Genesis 1:14-19

14 And God said, Let there be lights in the firmament of the heaven to divide the day from the night; and let them be for signs, and for seasons, and for days, and years:

15 And let them be for lights in the firmament of the heaven to give light upon the earth: and it was so.

16 And God made two great lights; the greater light to rule the day, and the lesser light to rule the night: he made the stars also.

17 And God set them in the firmament of the heaven to give light upon the earth,

18 And to rule over the day and over the night, and to divide the light from the darkness: and God saw that it was good.

19 And the evening and the morning were the fourth day.

---

[290] Gen. 1:3.
[291] Gen. 1:14.

Light was given for "signs, and for seasons, and for days, and for years." The Holy Spirit gives us wisdom concerning the days we live in so that we know what we ought to do (1 Chron. 12:32). These lights were set in the heavens to "rule over the day and over the night." The Holy Spirit convinces us in the ways of right judgment, letting us know the correct execution of God's will on earth through the light of revelation (Eph. 1:17-19; 5:8-11).

Oil
Olive oil comes from the squeezed fruit of the olive tree. Fruit trees sprang forth at the command of God on the third day (Gen. 1:11-13). Three is the number of divine completeness. The Lord is One—Father, Son, and Holy Ghost (Matt. 28:19). We need the anointing of the Holy Spirit to walk in all that God has for us.

Galatians 5:22-25
22 But the fruit of the Spirit is love, joy, peace, longsuffering, gentleness, goodness, faith,
23 Meekness, temperance: against such there is no law.
24 And they that are Christ's have crucified the flesh with the affections and lusts.
25 If we live in the Spirit, let us also walk in the Spirit.

The Golden Lampstand
The fruit trees sprang out of the dry ground, which the Lord made appear on the third day as well. He laced the land of the Edenic Havilah with veins of gold and called it good (Gen. 2:11-12). Along with being the number of divine completeness, three is also the number of complete testimony. "Every matter may be established by the testimony of two or **three** witnesses," Jesus said (Matt. 18:16 NIV, emphasis added). The Holy Spirit completes the testimony of God.

1 John 5:5-8
5 Who is he that overcometh the world, but he that believeth that Jesus is the Son of God?

6 This is he that came by water and blood, even Jesus Christ; not by water only, but by water and blood. And it is the Spirit that beareth witness, because the Spirit is truth.

7 For there are three that bear record in heaven, the Father, the Word, and the Holy Ghost: and these three are one.

8 And there are three that bear witness in earth, the spirit, and the water, and the blood: and these three agree in one.

Even as the golden lampstand in the holy place revealed the cherubim-embroidered veil (the body of Jesus, Heb. 10:20) and the showbread (the bread of Heaven, the word of God, John 6:41; Matt. 4:4), the Spirit reveals the truth of the written word and the Living Word. His presence in us empowers us to give full testimony of the gospel of grace.

Acts 1:8
But ye shall receive power, after that the Holy Ghost is come upon you: and ye shall be witnesses unto me both in Jerusalem, and in all Judaea, and in Samaria, and unto the uttermost part of the earth.

Dove
Doves were created on the fifth day along with all the other birds (Gen. 1:20-22). Five is the number of grace in Scripture. In His graciousness, the Lord provided five primary offerings for atonement, worship, and communion with God (Lev. 1-5). When Jesus ascended, He gave five primary ministry gifts to equip the church to grow up fully in Him (Eph. 4:8-15). There is a correlation between the character of the offerings and ministries that are worthy of meditation. I list them in Table 10.1 below, leaving it to the reader to delve deeper into their implications as the Spirit leads.

Offerings	**Ministries**
Burnt	Apostle
Grain	Teacher
Fellowship (peace)	Pastor
Sin	Evangelist
Guilt (trespass)	Prophet

Table 10.1

Jesus instructed us to be wise as serpents and pure as doves (Matt. 10:16). It is in the gracious purity of the Holy Spirit's dove leading that we offer our bodies as living sacrifices in holy, spiritual worship of God (Rom. 12:1).

Eagle

As stated above, birds were created on the fifth day. God in His grace delivered Israel's children from the bondage of Egypt. A nation of slaves marched out in five columns as a liberated army.

Exodus 13:18
But God led the people around by the way of the wilderness toward the Red Sea. And the people of Israel went up out of the land of Egypt equipped for battle. ESV

The Hebrew word translated "equipped for battle" in the verse above is *chamush* and means "arrayed for battle by fives."[292] The eagle is a bird of war, and it is through being strong in the grace of God that we can endure as good soldiers of Christ Jesus.

2 Timothy 2:1-3
1 Thou therefore, my son, be strong in the grace that is in Christ Jesus.
2 And the things that thou hast heard of me among many witnesses, the same commit thou to faithful men, who shall be able to teach others also.
3 Thou therefore endure hardness, as a good soldier of Jesus Christ.

The Cloud

Clouds are the visible presence of water in the air. They are part of "the waters which were above" in Genesis 1:7 and share with water the narrative sense of being eternal. But the *cumulonimbus capillatus,*

---

[292] *The Online Bible Thayer's Greek Lexicon and Brown Driver & Briggs Hebrew Lexicon*, Copyright © 1993, Woodside Bible Fellowship, Ontario, Canada.

the anvil-headed thundercloud (*'anan* in the Hebrew) makes its first appearance in Genesis 9:13 when God signified the Noahic covenant with the rainbow after the flood. Once again, we are reminded of the Holy Spirit as the Spirit of judgement who leads us into renewed covenant (Isa. 4:4-6).

These all are earthly things through which the Spirit instructs us about Himself. We can read, study, and ask as Nicodemus did. When we ask in faith, truly desiring, Jesus does not leave us on the earthly plane. He moves the conversations into the heavenly realm to carry our gaze upward and forward.

John 3:13-16
13 No one has ascended into heaven except he who descended from heaven, the Son of Man.
14 And as Moses lifted up the serpent in the wilderness, so must the Son of Man be lifted up,
15 that whoever believes in him may have eternal life.
16 "For God so loved the world, that he gave his only Son, that whoever believes in him should not perish but have eternal life. ESV

The One who came from heaven testified of Heaven's saving grace. The Father gave the Son as the perfect sacrifice for sin. Those who accept this in faith are granted eternal life through the Spirit. In the words of John the Baptist:

John 3:31-36
31 He who comes from above is above all. He who is of the earth belongs to the earth and speaks in an earthly way. He who comes from heaven is above all.
32 He bears witness to what he has seen and heard, yet no one receives his testimony.
33 Whoever receives his testimony sets his seal to this, that God is true.

34 For he whom God has sent utters the words of God, for he gives the Spirit without measure.

35 The Father loves the Son and has given all things into his hand.

36 Whoever believes in the Son has eternal life; whoever does not obey the Son shall not see life, but the wrath of God remains on him. ESV

The Father gave the Son the limitless supply of the Holy Spirit to pour life eternal into all who believe. All who have breath are in relationship with the Holy Spirit. He blows where He wills through our planet, convicting all of sin, righteousness, and judgment. Those who reject Him will not see life. But those who listen and obey come to drink from the fountain of life that flows from the throne of God.

Revelation 22:17
And the Spirit and the bride say, Come. And let him that heareth say, Come. And let him that is athirst come. And whosoever will, let him take the water of life freely.

The Holy Spirit is the third Person of the Godhead. He desires more than simply empowering us. He wants to embrace us and for us to embrace Him. He speaks to us in the gale and the gentle breeze, in the waterfall and winter's freeze. The heavens flash and light the altar's flame. As oil flows and lamps alight, He coaxes us with coos to eagle's flight. The thunders roar and the glory cloud glistens. The Creator speaks, we do well to listen.

I pray that the grace of the Lord Jesus Christ and the love of God and the fellowship of the Holy Spirit be with you.

ACKNOWLEDGEMENTS

ಬಿಂದ

This work would have been impossible without the generations of committed men and women who dedicated themselves to the study of the Word of God and the subsequent development and publishing of devotional works and study helps. I thank God for their gifts to us which allow us to stand on their shoulders while we grow in the faith.

Pastor Bobby Hill and the leadership of New Life Christian Fellowship as the twentieth century turned into the twenty-first are owed special thanks. It was this Christian community that first accepted me in the love of God as I emerged from the cul-de-sac of unorthodox Christianity where I spent much of my youth. They lovingly led my wife and me back into the greater body of Christ. In many ways, this book is the direct fruit of their faith and labor of love.

I am indebted to the saints of Maranatha Church, past and present, whose love for God, walk with Jesus, and attentiveness to the Holy Spirit are a continual inspiration to me. This work was developed and taught in the living laboratory that is our community. Thank you for your love and support over all these many years.

All writers need an editor and I was privileged to work with a great one. Thank you, Sherrill Fink, for your work on my drafts, for spurring me to continually bring greater clarity to the text, and your continual encouragement. I could not have done it without you.

No words would suffice to express love and gratefulness I have for my wife and children. They believe in me. They love me. Because of them, I am the wealthiest man I know.

Bibliography

❧❦

Brauch, Manfred T., *Abusing Scripture: The Consequences of Misreading the Bible*, Downers Grove: InterVarsity Press, 2009.

The Catholic Encyclopedia, "The Blessed Trinity", http://www.knight.org/advent/cathen/15047a.htm.

Chin, Kok-Yong, and Soelaiman Ima-Nirwana. "Olives and Bone: A Green Osteoporosis Prevention Option." Ed. Paul B. Tchounwou. *International Journal of Environmental Research and Public Health* 13.8 (2016):755, https://www.ncbi.nlm.nih.gov/pmc/articles/PMC4997441/.

Connor, Kevin J., *Interpreting the Symbols and Types: Completely revised and expanded edition*, Portland: BT Publishing, 1992.

Conner, Kevin J. and Malmin, Ken, *Interpreting the Scriptures*, Portland: Bible Temple Publishing, 1983.

Edersheim, Alfred, *The Temple: Its Ministries and Services*, *Updated Edition*, Peabody: Hendrickson Publishers, 1994.

Fernández-Real, José Manuel and others, "A Mediterranean Diet Enriched with Olive Oil is Associated with Higher Serum Total Osteocalcin Levels in Elderly Men at High Cardiovascular Risk." *The Journal of Clinical Endocrinology & Metabolism*, Volume 97, Issue 10, https://academic.oup.com/jcem/article-lookup/doi/10.1210/jc.2012-2221.

Gill, Frank B., *Ornithology*, New York: W. H. Freeman and Co., 1990.

Green, Arthur, *These Are the Words: A Vocabulary of Jewish Spiritual Life*, Woodstock: Jewish Lights Publishing, 1999.

Hagen, Susan, "The Mind's Eye," *Rochester Review* 74, no. 4 (2012), http://www.rochester.edu/pr/Review/V74N4/0402_brainscience.html.

House, H. Wayne, *Charts of Christian Theology & Doctrine*, Grand Rapids: Zondervan Publishing House, 1992.

Jewish Virtual Library, "Jewish Holidays: Shavu'ot," 2017, http://www.jewishvirtuallibrary.org/shavu-ot.

Larum, Nikolas, *The Blood of Jesus Christ: Its Life to the Body, Its Power for the Priesthood, and Its Purchase of the Bride*, Maitland: Xulon Press, 2005.

Missler, Chuck, *Personal Update – August 1995*, "One God or Three?" Coeur d'Alene: Koinonia House, Inc., 1996.

Murray, Andrew, *The Holiest of All*, New Kensington: Whitaker House, 1996.

O'Grady, Joan, *Early Christian Heresies*, New York: Barnes & Noble Books, 1985.

The Online Bible Thayer's Greek Lexicon and Brown Driver & Briggs Hebrew Lexicon, Ontario: Woodside Bible Fellowship, 1993.

Otis, Jr., George, *The Last of the Giants*, Grand Rapids: Baker Book House Co., 1991.

Pidwirny, Michael, *Fundamentals of Physical Geography (2nd Edition)*, 2008, http://www.physicalgeography.net/fundamentals/7p.html.

Robertson's Word Pictures in the New Testament, Electronic Database. Knoxville: Biblesoft, Inc., 2006.

Sattle, Helen Roney, *The Book of Eagles*, New York: Lothrop, Lee & Shepard Books, 1989.

Sclein, Miriam and Cromwell, Thomas Y., *Pigeons*, New York: Junior Books, 1989.

Switzer, Merebeth, *Nature's Children: Eagles*, Laval: Grolier Limited, 1985.

Tipler, Frank J., *The Physics of Immortality*, New York: Doubleday, 1994.

Tozer, A. W., *The Counselor: Straight Talk about the Holy Spirit from a 20th-Century Prophet* Christian Publications, Inc., 1993.

Unger, Merrill F., "Pillar of Cloud and Fire," *PC Study Bible: The New Unger's Bible Dictionary*, Originally published by Moody Press, Chicago, 1988.

The Wilson Bulletin—No. 100, 2017, https://sora.unm.edu/sites/default/files/journals/wilson/v029n03/p0164-p0165.pdf.

Wormer, Joe Van, *Eagles*, New York: E. P. Dutton, 1985.

ฅດຮ

213

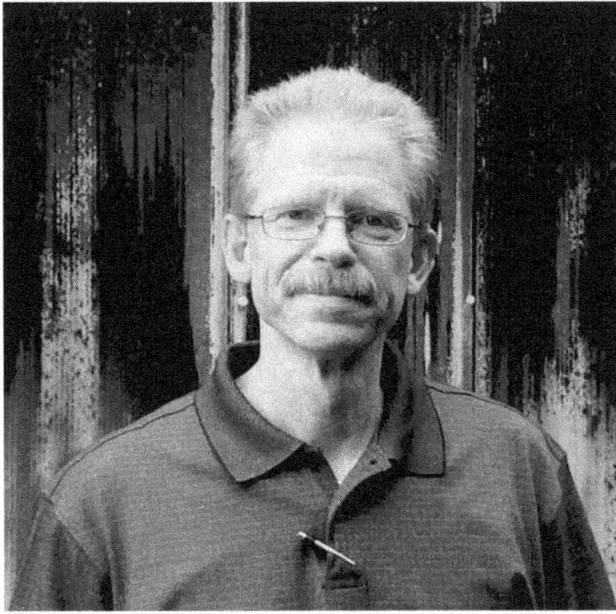

Nikolas Larum has been teaching the Bible to gatherings small and large, at home and abroad, for over thirty-five years. He has served as the pastor of Maranatha Church, a multi-generational house church in coastal Virginia, since 1994. A bi-vocational minister, Larum has worked as a government contractor and in the recycling industry. He lives with the wife of his youth and four of their children (and menagerie of pets) in Chesapeake, Virginia.